THOMAS HARDY

Thomas Hardy.
from a photograph by H. W. Barnett.

THOMAS HARDY
A CRITICAL STUDY
BY
LASCELLES ABERCROMBIE

New York

RUSSELL & RUSSELL

1964

FIRST PUBLISHED IN 1912
REISSUED, 1964, BY RUSSELL & RUSSELL, INC.
L. C. CATALOG CARD NO: 64—8920

PR
4754
.A2
1964

PRINTED IN THE UNITED STATES OF AMERICA

NOTE

MR. HARDY has kindly given me permission to use such quotations as I required for this study of his work. But it should be understood that the book contains nothing whatever that may be called "authorized"; it is simply my own reading of Mr. Hardy's stories and poems. Biography was no part of my intention. The book will scarcely appeal to those who are not already acquainted with its subject; but fortunately it is not extravagant to assume a very general knowledge of the works here considered. It was therefore easy to dispense with full descriptions of narrative material, with analyses of plots, and so on. I have simply attempted to criticize my private belief that Thomas Hardy's books are among the greatest things in our modern literature; and, more generally, to discuss not so much their exact "place," as the way they utter certain characteristics of modern consciousness. I am under considerable obligation to Mr. Arthur Ransome; by using his distinction between "kinetic" and "potential" language, the discussion of style in prose and poetry was very greatly facilitated. However, my own obligation is only a small part of what is due to Mr. Ransome from the science of criticism itself; for, now that this distinction of his has been formulated, I suppose its use can scarcely be avoided in any precise examination of diction.

Perhaps it may not be amiss if I express here a feeling which could not conveniently appear in the sequel: my deep sense of gratitude to Mr. Hardy, for many unforgettable experiences.

L. A.

CONTENTS

CHAPTER		PAGE
I.	INTRODUCTORY	11
II.	CHARACTERISTICS	25
III.	MINOR NOVELS	63
IV.	ANNEXES	76
V.	DRAMATIC FORM	97
VI.	EPIC FORM	129
VII.	THE POEMS	170
VIII.	THE DYNASTS	184

I

INTRODUCTORY

AMONG the arts, as among favourites at court in the old days, the latest comer has usually the most influence. For long enough the mind of man did pretty well without the service and flattery of the two most recently ennobled arts, Music and the Novel; but, now they have been taken into favour, it is, above all others, these two that have the say with their master. Their right to such a position is not to be disputed; for here, as elsewhere, the right to a position is no more than the power to maintain it, and there is no questioning the powers which Music and the Novel possess to-day. The arts, which enjoyed a former and, as some still think, a more deserved favour, are not, assuredly, so forgotten by their fortune as to be rebuked quite into dumbness; but their most manful partisans must perceive that their words are nothing so persuasive, nor so comfortable, nor so convenient to the mood of the time, as the speech of the two latest favourites. However, there is no shifty caprice in man's favouritism among the arts. Having listened for a good while to the doctrines of one, he, it seems, unconsciously wishes to try the counsel of another ; and this one he advances into his chief pleasure. It is surely fair dealing. But the new art will not hold itself there if man himself is to be a loser by the advancement ; if it cannot at least promise to be as courteous and as wise and as practical in the policy of his great affairs, as the art which preceded it in favour. We must suppose, judging from what history can see of such events in the past, that no art comes to be a vizier over the others with full immediate possession of all the capabilities man expects from such an officer ; and it looks as if man is always willing to give generous trial to a new vizier, and even to endure from him blunders in flattery and dangerous mistakes in persuasion, in the confident hope that the required capabilities will develop precision and depth by the mere training of the post. On the whole, the hope has found itself justified ; a crude, ungrown, unlikely art, by simply ousting from favour one full of serious experience and high speculation, has often itself become all as commanding as the art it displaced. And this is natural; for all the arts are of one family, and, like the Barmecides, need but the opportunity of the

INTRODUCTORY

king's favour to bring forth similar genius for pleasing and advising him.

According to our fable, then, the two commanding arts of the present, as far as favour goes, are also the two which we should specially expect to show development and "progress"; and, plainly, this is the case. But there is, in addition, something remarkable about the position held to-day by Music and Fiction; and it is this, that they have never held the position before. Man, for as long as he has truly been man, has no doubt always had them near him; but they have never before this present period of civilization been placed where poetry and sculpture and drama have so often been placed. We cannot here inquire into the reasons for this, nor draw any conclusions therefrom; our present business is to determine, if possible, whether man's confidence in artistic development has, as heretofore, been justified; whether, in fact, of these two new-comers to supremacy, the one in which we are here concerned has shown itself able to counsel man as greatly, as passionately and as seriously, and to flatter him as pleasantly and courageously, as the arts which have many times preceded it in the chief office.

For, as to music, the time of doubting has long ago gone by. A hundred years ago music proved itself as powerful a counsellor as any art has ever been; and since then, though it has done many bold things, it has added nothing to the nobility of its wisdom. But Fiction has had a slower growth; and it is still plausible to doubt whether man's spirit might not be better served by discarding this art in favour of one more experienced in the highest matters. Indeed, what has Fiction done in the highest matters? Take any great piece of poetry or sculpture or drama; and put any novel beside it. Is there not something which the latter too evidently lacks? And is this not the very thing which by its presence allows, and by its absence disallows, an art to take the highest place in man's service? Such questions are certainly plausible, provided that they refer not merely to the content, but to the whole manner and conduct of art. Nevertheless, this book will endeavour to maintain, that in our own time certain novels have been written which must be excluded from this general disapprobation of Fiction. It will be claimed for the Wessex Novels of Thomas Hardy that in them Fiction has achieved both a style and a substance that enable it to fulfil the gravest function of art—with the exception, perhaps, of the work of two foreign novelists, to fulfil this function for the first time. That this achievement is not for the most part perfectly understood, is very explic-

INTRODUCTORY

able; for the novel has no history of similar achievement to help our appreciation. If it were, for example, sculpture that concerned us, we could refer back to Michelangelo, to Pheidias, to the Pyramid Age. But for judging Fiction, there is no such assistance from bygones. It will be convenient, therefore, before examining Thomas Hardy's work in any detail, to set down generally what is meant by this lofty claim.

In the first place, it does not necessarily assert this author to be greater in personal genius than, say, Cervantes or Defoe, Fielding or Balzac. Nor need the claim be sustained by any pretence that the Wessex Novels are superior in all qualities to every other book of the kind. In humour, tragedy, narrative, psychological imagination, and spacious setting, Mr. Hardy's finest novels are altogether admirable. But other novels have at least equalled them in these matters. The thing is, however, that if Fiction is to take an equal place among the most aspiring of the arts—if it is to be more than a wholesome and laudable amusement, more than a remedy for severe hours, if it is to be a notable increase of power in man's endeavour for consciously delighted life—these matters must be no more than a means to an end. Mr. Hardy has deliberately and masterfully applied them to that end with more evident purpose and larger success than any other novelist. Just as the crude material of human living must be shaped artistically into the qualities above mentioned, so these very qualities must be the material submitted to the shaping of a higher artistic power, presiding and domineering over the whole. The activity of this higher power is what has given to such arts as sculpture and drama a greatness of complete achievement which Fiction was, on the whole, quite unable to rival until the Wessex Novels appeared; it may be called the metaphysical power of art. The idea requires a little elaboration.

Man's intercourse with the world is necessarily formative. His experience of things outside his consciousness is in the manner of a chemistry, wherein some energy of his nature is mated with the energy brought in on his nerves from externals, the two combining into something which exists only in, or perhaps we should say closely around, man's consciousness. Thus what man knows of the world is what has been *formed* by the mixture of his own nature with the streaming in of the external world. This formative energy of his, reducing the in-coming world into some constant manner of appearance which may be appreciable by consciousness, is most

INTRODUCTORY

conveniently to be described, it seems, as an unaltering *imaginative desire*:[1] desire which accepts as its material, and fashions itself forth upon, the many random powers sent by the world to invade man's mind. That there is this formative energy in man may easily be seen by thinking of certain dreams; those dreams, namely, in which some disturbance outside the sleeping brain (such as a sound of knocking or a bodily discomfort) is completely formed into vivid trains of imagery, and in that form only is presented to the dreamer's consciousness. This, however, merely shows the presence of the active desire to shape sensation into what consciousness can accept; the dream is like an experiment done in the isolation of a laboratory; there are so many conflicting factors when we are awake that the events of sleep must only serve as a symbol or diagram of the intercourse of mind with that which is not mind—intercourse which only takes place in a region where the outward radiations of man's nature combine with the irradiations of the world. Perception itself is a formative act; and all that construction of sensation into some orderly, coherent idea of the world is a further activity of the

[1] "The Will to Form" would perhaps suit some people better. In this, of course, the famous "Will to Power" is included, much as theory includes practice. There must necessarily be some formative inspiration behind achieved power.

central imaginative desire. But what is important for our purpose to note here is, that after all this has been done there remains an overplus of imaginative desire; man, it seems, has more of it in him than is required for acceptably presenting externality to consciousness; there remains some desire which is still unused, unsatisfied, unembodied. And the desire is urgent to be used, embodied, thereby satisfied. This is the function of art: to satisfy, by embodying, man's overplus of imaginative desire. Art is created, and art is enjoyed, because in it man may find himself completely expressing and exercising those inmost desires which in ordinary experience are by no means to be completely expressed. Life has at last been perfectly formed and measured to man's requirements; and in art man knows himself truly the master of his existence. It is this sense of mastery which gives man that raised and delighted consciousness of self which art provokes.

In art, then, man is the master of his being, in so far, at least, as that which is most profoundly human in him has found triumphant activity. It is consequently in art that his consciousness of self is most positive and most enjoyed. But there are degrees in the mastery, and therefore in the consequence. The whole overplus of

INTRODUCTORY

imaginative desire is not exercised unless the art is of the very highest. Until that art is reached, we may have æsthetic formation of the pleasure in existence, of the relations, whether of conflict or attraction, between human individuals, between man and society, between man and nature; of particular problems in the moral and practical difficulties wherewith man's life is beset; we may even have the paradoxical æsthetic formation of deep desires made always futile by the external destiny, able only to keep a courageous front to their futility; we may have all this contained in art by successive inclusions, one within the other; and yet we shall not have the highest of art. There remains unsatisfied still something of the imaginative desire; in such art man has not yet altogether attained to mastery. The highest art must have a metaphysic; the final satisfaction of man's creative desire is only to be found in æsthetic formation of some credible correspondence between perceived existence and a conceived absoluteness of reality. Only in such art will the desire be employed to the uttermost; only in such art, therefore, will conscious mastery seem complete. And Thomas Hardy, by deliberately putting the art of his fiction under the control of a metaphysic, has thereby made the novel capable of the highest service to man's consciousness—made it truly the equal of drama and sculpture.

For if the metaphysic be there at all, it must be altogether in control; it would not do to have it as an intellectual burthen foisted on the rest; that would be but poorly, as by an afterthought, to satisfy this final artistic desire. The metaphysic will be something (as it is in Hardy's work) which can only be expressed by the *whole* of the art which contains it; everything will conspire to symbolize it to us. It will not therefore be something which may easily be expressed in words; such metaphysic should belong to philosophy; when Mr. Hardy does attempt overtly to express it, he weakens his work. It is to be more a feeling than an idea, an ethical metaphysic rather than an intellectual; somewhat like that of Anaximander,[1] to whom the differentiation of limited existence from the primal unlimited being seemed a moral transgression, an offence against the majesty of boundlessness, justly punished by inevitable death; or, a better instance, like the terrible metaphysic expressed in Michelangelo's statue called "Dawn." That Mr. Hardy's metaphysic

[1] Philosophy is also a satisfaction, by complete employment, of the overplus of man's imaginative desire; but it has become distinguished from art as the satisfaction given primarily through the intellect. In Anaximander's time, however, a philosophical metaphysic was not yet sharply distinguishable from an artistic one.

INTRODUCTORY

is also like these in being tragical could not be avoided; for who knows better than he how the senseless process of the world for ever contradicts the human will? Indeed, tragedy, and especially a tragic metaphysic, is the one remedy good for this desolating knowledge; more will be said of this in the next chapter.

The notion of artistic mastery over existence is one that is common nowadays in criticism; but many, too easily inspired by Nietzsche, are apt to use it narrowly, in the dangerous spirit of doctrinaires. It seems to be thought that there should be some strict choice in the materials of art; in the case of Fiction, only "masterful," "aristocratic" natures should be exhibited. This, of course, is nonsense, an absurd mistaking of the way in which great art does indeed infect him who enjoys it with a conscious mastery over existence. It matters not at all what material be used, so long as it is used to give the complete satisfaction, the final employment, to imaginative desire; for that brings consciousness to its highest sense of mastery. What does matter is the form given to the material; it can only be by a rigorous and exquisite order that the metaphysic of art, the ethically formed sense of temporal things irresistibly wielded by eternal things, can become expressed and symbolized throughout the whole of a work of art. There are no novels like Thomas Hardy's for perfection of form; and this is the sign of the inward perfection the novel has taken from his hands.

It was important to insist, even at the risk of some tedium, on what Mr. Hardy has done for the novel. He has made it adequate for the high position to which man has latterly elevated it among the arts. To go back to the fabulous allegory with which this chapter began, it is now not only capable of that judicious flattery required of a royal confidant, but also capable of giving the most serious advice that man's occasions can demand. These two functions of viziership, indeed, have become inextricable. The flattery of art begins in rendering the mere delight in taking part in existence; but it comes to a strong persuasion to accept, and at last to delight in, the tragic ground-bass which keenly civilized consciousness always hears accompanying the tune of the world.[1] This delight in tragedy must, naturally, be of an æsthetic nature; its perfection can only come from giving some form of art to the relation between known experience and a conception of originating reality; it can only come, in fact, from the

---

[1] See the famous description of Egdon Heath with which *The Return of the Native* opens, especially the fifth, sixth, and eighth paragraphs.

INTRODUCTORY

ultimate satisfaction of imaginative desire. It is by no means necessary that the consequent metaphysic of an art should be universally accepted outside the art. The fact that we cannot nowadays altogether accept the metaphysic of Prometheus Bound has little result on the nobility of its effect. We have a right to demand no more than that while we are immersed in an art, and giving ourselves up to it, everything therein shall work together to make us at the conclusion apprehend the metaphysic dominating the whole, a perfect congruence of the rhythm of seen things with an imagined rhythm of unseen reality; thereby the human formative desire reaches some finality of expression; the faculty which underlies cognition (its imperfect activity) attains in such art to the perfection of activity.

We have not yet the perspective which will enable us to say how much of this achievement is due to the personal genius of Thomas Hardy, and how much to the spirit of the time. But certainly the achievement sorts well with the latter. If ever fiction could arrive at the full spiritual stature of an art, this would be the time for it; for to-day, when the mind has little safety in tradition, an art which can achieve formation and human symbolization of some speculative metaphysic is obviously required.

THOMAS HARDY

Thomas Hardy, however, has not done this merely as a novelist; though the quality of his contribution to fiction, to the dominant art of the day, needed special emphasis in this introduction. It may well turn out that, in absolute value, his greatest work is *The Dynasts*, which is described as an "epic drama"; but it will be convenient in the sequel to treat of this tremendous thing separately from the rest, though it is certainly, in spirit, the climax of all the works—novels, short stories, and poems—which had preceded it in publication.

II

CHARACTERISTICS

It will not be supposed that the contention just put forward is meant to include all Thomas Hardy's novels; but since we find that, where the contention is fully justified, the novels are works of tragic purport, we may conclude that a tragic apprehension of the world is a profound characteristic of Hardy's mind: for these are the novels in which his mind has been most completely liberated into expression. The obvious quality of Hardy's tragedy is that it does not begin in the persons who are most concerned in it; it is an invasion into human consciousness of the general tragedy of existence, which thereby puts itself forth in living symbols. We assuredly do not feel Hardy's tragic characters to be mere puppets jerked by a malicious fate; were it so, indeed, they would miss an essential condition of tragedy. There is a well-known Russian symphony which is supposed to exhibit the idea of a supernal fate enjoying its leisure by deliberately wrecking human happiness; and some hasty criticism has sometimes assumed this sort of sinister interference as the fate in Hardy's tragedy. But he is far enough from such savage or childish metaphysics. Neither has he anything comparable with the moralized destiny of Greek tragedy, ready to avenge any violence to the prescribed symmetry of mortal affairs; nor is his fate at all like the figure which unexpectedly and dreadfully "knocks at the door," but nevertheless can be overcome by an exultation in C major. It is, indeed, not an activity at all, this tragic fate in Hardy's novels; it is a condition of activity. The general, measureless process of existence, wherein all activity is included, cares nothing, in working itself out, for the needs and desires of individual existence; the only relation between the two (but it is an utterly unavoidable relation) is that in the long run the individual must obey the general. The main stream of tendency has an ultimate power over all the vortices within it. It is a state of affairs which is, of course, especially unfortunate for consciously sensitive human creatures who have the additional ill-luck to be firmly persuaded that their desires must have some creative value, some power of modifying the worldly process. In fact, the very faculty of formative desire which in art actually does master the world, into a sort of cognition

CHARACTERISTICS

sublimated by will and feeling, is, in Hardy's art, the staple of his tragedy; since without this individual desire, which ordinary (i.e. extra-artistic) experience must leave inevitably unsatisfied, existence could not be supposed to have an altogether tragic significance. Human desire must therefore be at best an irony; when completely wrought into artistic form it must appear as tragedy. This conception is characteristic of all Hardy's work; though quite evident only in the greatest, the most tragic novels, it underlies also even those which may properly be called comedy. We never feel the characters to be isolated in a purely human world; the conditions of their being, and their being itself, are always *engaged* (as Hardy's architectural language might put it) with an immense background of measureless fatal processes, a moving, supporting darkness more or less apparent; it may be only hinted at, but it is always to be felt.

In appears that, in prose fiction, such a conception as this may be tolerably expressed only through the symbolism of a human action; Hardy's triumph is that he has, in several instances, made of this limited symbolism a completely efficient expression. But where the verbal medium is the far more cogent one of poetry, a closer and more direct formation of this basic idea becomes easily tolerable. Accordingly, we find that in *The Dynasts*, as well as in several lyrics, what in the novels is only a condition of activity, has come to be imagined as itself an activity, even as an anthropomorphic activity. There is no supposition of a fate which attempts to dislocate or interfere with earthly business; simply, the unswerving perpetual necessity of the world becomes the utterance of some power which is humanly appreciable; some explanation—that is, some formation—is even attempted of its ruthlessness, its fearful carelessness of what it inflicts on harmless individual desire. Thus, in " Ἀγνώστῳ Θεῷ," it is imagined as a species of labour, but of something

> "labouring all-unknowingly,
> *Like one whom reveries numb.*"

This may not be very satisfactory to the philosopher; but poetically it is a remarkable idea, and in *The Dynasts* is used with extraordinary effect. The chapter on that poem will deal with this matter more narrowly.

This basic conception may possibly be called pessimism. But it is pessimism very different from that splenetic kind professed by diseases like Strindberg or Huysmans. For it is capable of tragedy; and tragedy is not, as the newspapers seem to think, something just sorrowful or distressing; it is a unity of several elements, and

CHARACTERISTICS

that which is grievous is but one of them. It is true that in Hardy's later work some suggestions are developed which are undoubtedly and dismally pessimistic. One of the worst is that horrible suicidal small boy in *Jude the Obscure*, who was "the outcome of new views of life," and typified "the coming universal wish not to live." Similar, but less painful, is the description of Jude himself: "He was the sort of man who was born to ache a good deal before the fall of the curtain upon his unnecessary life should signify that all was well with him again."[1] But these are not tragic feelings, for there is no tragedy where there is no resistance. Jude does indeed ache; but his resistance is magnificent, and so also is his tragedy. His death was certainly desirable in the end, but not until he had passionately striven. However, these genuinely pessimistic notions are flaws in a tragic imagination of life; but not here very considerable.

Given, then, such a basic conception of necessity as I have been indicating, the first thing required in order to turn it into tragedy is human resistance. Without resistance, indeed, the current of necessity could never be symbolized at all; just as an electric current must

[1] "Lieta no, ma sicura
Dell' antico dolor."—*Leopardi*.

pass through some resistance to become apparent in incandescence. And tragedy plainly requires further, that the resistance be of some nobility and dignity; for tragedy must be a thing enjoyable in itself. Even though we foresee, as we do in most of Hardy's great novels, that a towering and laudable desire is doomed to be brought level with futility, we profoundly enjoy the brave quality of the assertion of the desire. A life abject in sorrow is nothing enjoyable, therefore nothing tragical. Henchard, Tess, and Jude, the three characters in the Wessex Novels who endure the most pitiless destiny, are never in the least abject. This destiny, however, this destroying, or levelling, or assimilating power, is not merely external to the characters who contend with it; that would be precluded by Hardy's characteristic conception of necessity. There is, certainly, a good deal of external compulsion in the working out of Hardy's plots; and it sometimes takes the form of coincidence. So long as the coincidence is credible, as it always is in the Wessex Novels, there can be no objecting to it; something of the kind is no doubt necessary to the artistic formation of experience. Such external pressure, however, is always far less important to the significance of the whole than the interior conflict. The main, ruthless stream of tendency,

CHARACTERISTICS

which the characters must in the end obey, exhibits itself not only around but in the characters themselves; only thus could they symbolize the basic conception of Hardy's tragedy. They have in them some weakness, disability, inherited instinct, or perhaps some error in the assertion of their strength, which inevitably becomes the chance for the power of the world finally to assert itself against them. This is more pathetic, because more natural, than any tragic interference from the outside; but Hardy always knows how to mitigate it by an exquisite tenderness, a justice of mercy, towards his own creations. It is especially noticeable in the case of his women. They are, on the whole, disturbing and even sinister agents in the stories; but no one would think of blaming them for that; it is their fate, not their fault—except, perhaps, in the case of Arabella in *Jude the Obscure*, the one woman to whom Hardy seems to show animosity. Neither do they exist as personalities chiefly by virtue of male affection for them, as most writers who have believed in the sinister efficiency of women have tried to make out. They do not simply form a passive characterless nucleus, round which male desire crystallizes in the form of imagined perfection, to become in the end distracted by finding there is nothing in the reality of womanhood answering to the ideal.¹ Hardy's women exist entirely in their own right; and even the ruinous fine ladies in *Two on a Tower* and *The Woodlanders* are easily forgiven for their sufferings, and their helplessness as the agents of a tragic destiny to which they themselves must submit.

It hardly needs to be remarked, that true tragic art also requires substantiality of material; that is, it must be embodied in persons entirely credible. For this, observation may be the first thing necessary; but it is not the most important. The process of "getting inside other people's skins" is a very subsidiary part of characterization. It does, indeed, narrowly exercise the power out of which all characterization really comes, the power of psychological imagination, stimulated by the gestures and other externals of conduct which have been observed. But mere observation is a small thing in the fashioning of such characters as Michael Henchard or Sue Bridehead: lucid, consistent, full of profound but clearly seen energies, yet capable of exhibiting actions that could hardly have been predicted, although, when they do occur,

---

¹ This is true of the novels. The poems, however, give at least one clear expression (*The Well-Beloved*) and several suggested ones, to this notion, the ironical counterpart of ideal or Platonic love. In the novel which is also called *The Well-Beloved*, the point is, that the idealized women are not nonentities, but insist on asserting individual personality.

CHARACTERISTICS

they evidently agree with the rest of the character, unexpectedly confirming it; such actions as Sue's jumping out of window to avoid her husband, or Henchard's pinioning one of his arms when he prepared for a fatal wrestle with the hated Farfrae. Such characters are the work, not of observation, but of a great psychological imagination, self-controlled by precisely the same sense of form as that which controls the whole action. There is a kind of characterization which is entirely made of evident consistency; this is the kind that produces the "types" of Jonson and Dickens—unquestionably a noble kind. But in it the power of observation is merely improved, energized, by the finer power of psychological imagination, the latter being controlled by the former. On the contrary, the characters of writers like Hardy completely dissolve what has been observed in the more eager, more exciting power of imagination. If this be not controlled by a masterful sense of form, such characters will probably consist simply of supple vagaries, as indeed they do in many plays of the Elizabethan period, the world's richest treasury, so far, of psychological imagination. But in the greatest playwrights of that period, and in Thomas Hardy and a few other novelists, the characterization is rigorously managed by the necessity of form; so that what is seen of a character, however unexpected, or even contradictory, must always be felt as the varying process of some withdrawn but perfectly defined and controlled source of personal nature.

There is a special kind of characterization that is sufficiently rare to be noted; it is characterization *in groups;* the invention of a set of persons who, while retaining marked and consistent individuality, combine into a group which is itself a consistent piece of psychology, a kind of communal personality including the individuals. The Wessex Novels have two exquisite instances of this, both used as backgrounds of contrasting comment to the main action: the unforgettable group of rustics in *Far from the Madding Crowd*, and—a smaller group, only pathetically humorous, but perfectly devised, an invention of as sweet a sadness as anything in literature—the group of milkmaids at Talbothays in *Tess of the D'Urbervilles*. This faculty of grouped psychology also appears, in a less conspicuous degree, in *Under the Greenwood Tree*, *The Mayor of Casterbridge*, and fitfully in the other stories.

It is likely that the remaining essential characteristic of tragedy which is now to be considered —the characteristic of form—is the one which gives the technique of Hardy's art its greatest opportunity. Without doubt, it was fortunate

CHARACTERISTICS

that a writer dealing in fundamental propositions so nearly approaching to pessimism (occasionally even, as has been pointed out, passing over into pessimism), should have been gifted with such an extraordinary power of artistic form; without this, the great quality of human resistance in his art could hardly have been enough to make a tragic matter of his conception of life and the world. How the power of form effects this, is easily explicable. For tragedy—it is a simple thing sometimes forgotten in theories—whatever else it may be, must, in some way or another, be profoundly enjoyable. And the formative desire —the desire (it has many names) for shapeliness, order, symmetry, completeness, significance, definiteness—is the hungriest lust the spirit possesses, and one whose satisfaction yields the deepest enjoyment. For this reason; its nourishment increases, and adds a sense of delighted mastery to, self-consciousness. By means of this formative desire, consciousness has all its commerce with the world. But the endless welter of the world, however formed to cognition and idea, will not itself thoroughly feed the desire. That can only be done by an artistic vision of the world, the representation of a world finally controlled into the form desired by the human spirit. Then, while we are spectators, and while clear memory of the spectacle lasts, self-consciousness is delighted with mastery, with the sense of perfect control achieved; the whole event of life, under such conditions, is to be enjoyed, even the tragical event of life; even an art which has for subject this very desire for order and justice baffled eternally in the affairs of earthly destiny, even such an art will give profound enjoyment, if its conduct, the manner of its representing, greatly pleases this inveterate desire.

Such an art is Thomas Hardy's. External form is a thing sufficiently noticeable in itself to be considered separately, and it is most conveniently to be so considered; although, as was suggested in the first chapter, it is inseparable from a formal conception of the subject. Form in art is not an imposition from without, not a thrusting of material into an arbitrary circumference; it is the result of a willing obedience, given by all the materials, to a presiding interest. And the result is a perfect separation from the surrounding disorder of the world. The common bent of all the lines of interest, all tending to "come full circle," will suffice to give the art its completed boundary. Completeness of roundure, of enclosure, is certainly required for great artistic formality; for if the periphery of a work of art be not closed in the work itself, if it can only be completed in the supposition of the spectator,

CHARACTERISTICS

perfect ease of attention is missing, and consequently also that surrounding quiescence in the spectator's mind which the sense of achieved mastery needs in order to become absolute and unquestioning. This is, of course, most naturally evident in arts wherein form is a visible pattern. The Athenian statue of Harmodius and Aristogeiton, for instance, splendid and exciting though it be, consists of lines of interest which all lead to something outside itself; the containing curve of interest is a parabola, which must be violently closed in the attention of the spectator, by supposing Hipparchus, the victim of that superb anger. The thing has not been isolated from the world, which means that formative control is incomplete. Whereas the Discobolus, a statue of much lower emotional significance, gives nevertheless a more certain sense of mastery, because no line in it has any tendency to lead either mind or eye outside the orderly system of the whole; everything bends towards something in the system; the whole thing achieves a precise circumference, and is a detached completed sphere of artistic command over life. But an exactly similar sensation is caused by the greatest of the Wessex Novels. They are detached and separate, held within formal boundaries made by the always inward-curving tendency of the lines whereon attention is led; from beginning to end nothing occurs to seduce interest away from the order of the whole. And form of this kind, when it governs such great passions and largely working characters and unruly conflicts as Hardy gives us, is more than a fine satisfaction; it is itself an exhilaration, not easily paralleled in the art of fiction hitherto, perhaps only in the art of Flaubert and Turgenev. Plot is, of course, included in form; and the lucid intricacy of Hardy's plots, their richness of incident, yet the complete absence of squandering in them—these obvious qualities have roused admiration from the first. The smallest occurrence is to be marked; for one feels the strict governance of form so strongly—though doubtless unconsciously, until we have gone far enough in the book to see its shape evidently making—that nothing seems capable of being insignificant, of failing to influence the process of the whole. This feeling is probably what many have described as the sense of fatality in Hardy's novels; it is simply a tribute to their form. Hardy delights in setting a great disturbing train of events on their way by means of a trivial or ludicrous beginning; Tess's tragedy, for instance, is set going by an antiquary's pedantic whim of addressing "plain Jack Durbeyfield, the haggler," as Sir John D'Urberville; and even the immense business of *The Dynasts* really

CHARACTERISTICS

all begins in King George's ridiculous pigheaded refusal to correspond with Napoleon as an equal. It is hardly necessary to mention similar examples of incidental events, occurring near the beginning of the story, which the sense of masterful formality in the work compels us to take at far more than their face value. Oak's chance meeting with Fanny Robin in the darkness is striking enough to serve us here. "Gabriel's fingers alighted on the young woman's wrist. It was beating with a throb of tragic intensity. He had frequently felt the same quick, hard beat in the femoral artery of his lambs when overdriven." The brief description of this meeting does not differ in texture from the occurrences which surround it; yet it is impossible not to perceive here some vague significance of tragedy. And the particular interest thus excited gradually weaves itself into the story until it becomes one of the master-strands; it is like a theme in music, which increases from its first quiet statement, through a persistent suggestion of counterpoint to other more evident themes, until at last it emerges into domination over the rest, in that greatly pathetic moment when Bathsheba uncovers the dead body of her innocent rival. The slow curving of several lines of interest, into such a unity of climax as this, gives a sense of an almost physical beauty of form. Again, in *The Mayor of Casterbridge*, the scene in the tent of the furmity-seller is an obvious beginning of tragedy; but the economy which gives the haggish furmity-seller herself a further crucial intervention at two moments in Henchard's tragedy, produces a wonderful sense of perfect formality. All these instances belong to the special kind of form called plot; but strictness of plot is, with Hardy, only a sign of strictness of general form. This is where he has so far proved to be beyond imitation. A closely wrought plot, at once rich and economical, is not a thing that needs to be copied from anyone; it is too obviously desirable. But attempts have been made to reproduce Hardy's effect of a passionate, intricate, complete human event thrown against the simplicity and deliberateness of the earth; to reproduce also the marriage of these elements into a metaphysical unity, "elix'd of all." And it is just in the strict coherence of general form that these attempts have so far failed of the desired effect. The plots have been well invented; the contrasting background of earth well described; the metaphysic tolerably conceived. But that incomparable fusion of the elements has been grievously missing, and therewith the whole effect. It is not a case for recipes; no ingenious compounding of analysed ingredients will serve

CHARACTERISTICS

this turn, but only a most unusual formative imagination, able to devise a complete system of human and unhuman things, which will supply from its own resources all required relationships, and become insphered by its own firm shapeliness, an ordered fusion of control isolated from the world of half-control and imperfect form. The stock instance of the chemical mingling of human with unhuman stuff in the Wessex Novels, is the umber grain of Egdon Heath which runs through *The Return of the Native;* the potency issuing darkly out of that space of desolation, and staining with inevitable tragedy the persons that move within it. And to say that the characters seem unable to escape from that queer potency, that they are strangely grasped by its subtle compulsion, is merely to say that the art which contains them is a thing complete in itself, perfectly supplying its own relationships, isolated by the strength of its form from the rest of the world.

Hardy's manhood began with artistic training; and with training in the art which is the type, for all the others, of severity of form—ecclesiastical architecture. For this is an art whose existence is unthinkable without absolute separation, by formality, from natural disorder. That such training is the cause of Hardy's success in controlling fiction to completely unified form, is an assertion which perhaps only a modern scientific biographer would support. Still, though this success comes from a native endowment—simply from an exceptional vigour of man's peculiar courage, the formative will—and might very probably have managed without a training in real (instead of in metaphorical) architectonics; yet such a training could hardly have been anything but wonderfully fortunate. It must have made the formative will conscious of its own powers; strengthened the assurance which it requires for liberated, masterful enjoyment of itself; finally made it incapable of that timidity which so remarkably cripples a deal of the drama, fiction, and music of to-day. Against that timidity—call it "realism" or "impressionism" or what you will—the Wessex Novels stand, a great rebuke; and the inevitable reaction against it, which should be beginning its heyday before the twentieth century is well past its third climacteric, will certainly see in Hardy's consistent achievement a most corroborative prophecy.

It may be thought that there has so far been an undue insistence on the tragic elements in Hardy's work. But we have not only the novels to consider. In these, to be sure, taking them as a whole, the tragedy might perhaps be considered as a characteristic of less than paramount

CHARACTERISTICS

importance; though never as a subordinate characteristic. It is evident, however, that the epic-drama of *The Dynasts* must be added to the novels if we are to have Hardy's complete speculation over life. And the effect of *The Dynasts*, with its great drama of human bewilderment persistently belittled by the background of tragic metaphysic, is unquestionably to make the tragedy in the novels stand out as their real purport; I mean that, after reading *The Dynasts*, we are bound to emphasize, in our recollection of the novels as a whole, that portion of their substance which plainly confirms the main tendency of the epic-drama; since in this great poem Hardy's idea of the world has evidently achieved its deepest candour of expression. But next to the tragedy of his work, and all that this implies, the greatest characteristics are no doubt those which would first appeal to the desultory reader of Hardy's books —their humour, and their beautiful pictures of country life and countryside. These never appear as ornamental foils to brighten the tragedy; though their contrasting effect has had a good deal to do with the admiration they have received. They are auxiliary expressions of the main dominating spirit of Hardy's work, whose thorough expression proves in the long run to be tragic. The English temper, as may be seen from its drama, its most instinctive utterance, prefers an art which can press into one obedience a number of very diverse elements; and for the sake of the diversity it is willing even to risk the effective control of a single presiding interest—as may also be seen in our drama. But Hardy never appears to run this risk; his humour and his country life have no tendency to become mere agreeable "relief"; and *Far from the Madding Crowd*, which elaborates the utmost diversity of material, gives as strong an impression of singleness of inmost motive as the unaltering, steadily increasing tragedy of *Jude the Obscure*. And it was therefore only to be expected that these auxiliary modes of expression—the humour and the rusticity—should become less evident, or at least less evidently contrasting, as the tragic expression becomes more insistent and more effective. The humour lessens noticeably, and its irony turns harsh and bitter; the background of nature seems to exist chiefly as a spectacular variation of human moods.

Humour is the least analysable of qualities. A good part of those delicious rural conversations in the Wessex Novels seems to appeal by the mere force of *naïveté;* the disconcerting candour of minds that simply accept, without gloss, the universal things of which culture is discreetly shy; at the same time labouring the significance of things that cause a by no means universal concern. The deputation of Mellstock quire, which waits on the new vicar, is astonished when he pities the gentle idiocy of skeletal Thomas Leaf; the poor fool is "silly by nater and could never get fat," and " Bless you, he don't mind it a bit, if you don't, sir"; what is the good of regretting that a man was born with half his wits? But when the vicar's chin bursts out bleeding where his razor had slipt, then something has happened which is worth discussing. There is always amusement in this kind of thing; but a mind habitually using it needs to have some unusual depth of sympathy in it, if such humour is to avoid a touch of sneering. Hardy seldom lacks sympathy for his characters; and his rustics are especially dear to him. He gives them something firm and oddly dignified behind their plentiful absurdity. Not only his naturals have it; but even his silly old men, Joseph Poorgrass and Grandfer Cantle, have that in them which makes laughter stop short of sneering. We laugh at these country folks' expressions, sometimes chiefly because it is so evidently laborious to them to express themselves at all. Their lives seem to go inwardly in such a way that words are of scant use to them; and when it comes to giving thought some outward shape of words, they endeavour to contrive this by a sort of general attack on language. They hope that a great many inappropriate phrases will somehow suggest the appropriate thought. And even while they are so entertaining us, we are feeling that their lives are more significant than speech can ever be. Their thought is not like that of the starved brains of townees, too poor to supply language with its material; it is too full of an undisturbed wealth that they do not quite know how to handle. But after all, the epithet that is commonly applied to Hardy's humour is the best for it; it is Shakespearean. In richness, in energy, in absurdity, in disconcertingness, it comes nearer to Shakespeare's than any other; and especially is it near to Shakespeare's in keeping, after all such lists of qualities have been made out, its essential quality unanalysed.

Hardy has nothing like wit in his writings; nothing successful, at any rate. His humour is altogether a property of his rustics, and his cultivated people are not noticeably entertaining, whether they try for wit or humour. The fact is typical of the limitation of his art in its material, one of its most remarkable characteristics. In his finest tragedy, as well as in his vividest humour, he is pretty strictly bound within a quite definite class of persons; though it is a class, certainly, which has so much possi-

CHARACTERISTICS

bility of human variety in it that there is no question of this limitation crippling his art at all. Indeed, it is hardly felt as a limitation except when he is working outside this class. Rustics, in a wide sense of the word—persons who win their living by some direct dealing with the earth—form the natural material of his art. This kind of humanity has been fashioned by him into an æsthetic language of profound expressiveness; but persons of culture, refinement, mental artifice, do not prove for him a biddable medium. No one, to be sure, would ever deplore the lack in his novels of a background of delicate or polite manners; the books are too splendidly decorated with the vivid manners and elemental habits of rusticity for that. The tremendous force in the slow lives of country folks has never been so shrewdly nor so unostentatiously exhibited as in the Wessex Novels. It is kept so quiet, though its presence is so plainly and so constantly to be felt, that when it leaps out undisguised into a sort of suddenly furious candour (as in those scenes of wild, tireless, all-night dancing), the effect is like a theophany.

But should this so obvious limitation to one firmly defined range of human material be considered in theory as a serious disability in Hardy's fiction? If we admit that the success of his work depends on strict choice of a certain kind of society, does that mean that we must admit his failure to be a " universal " artist ? It seems to me that to say yes to these questions is to confuse the material of art with the art itself. A writer may deal with a much more multifarious humanity than Hardy does, and yet, I think, fall far short of being as universal in the result as he is. Taking physical and mental experience as the condition of art, what the artist has to do is to form this condition into some image of spiritual experience, which for the most part is spiritual desire, its good or bad success. And if, as Hardy does, he form an image capable of representing some spiritual experience which may truly be called universal—if he represent thereby some serious variety of the spiritual attitude to worldly fate which is inevitable to-day—it seems that we have no right to quarrel with the condition, however confined, wherein that result was formed. Moreover, in the matter of sheer art, this limitation of his turns out a decided advantage. It is a capital instance of art's honourable old trick of making a virtue of necessity. No doubt the limitation of Hardy's most characteristic self-expression to the lives and manners and minds of country folk was, originally, an obedience to some obscure necessity of his mind. But consider the series of novels in which his genius

CHARACTERISTICS

is at its greatest, finding its most unquestionable utterance; consider, that is to say, this series: *Under the Greenwood Tree, Far from the Madding Crowd, The Mayor of Casterbridge, The Return of the Native, The Woodlanders, Tess of the D'Urbervilles*, and *Jude the Obscure*. These seven books naturally group themselves into a single whole; the series seems itself to become a work of art. And this is mainly because the uniformity of their chief material gives to these seven books as a whole that *isolation* which is the primary æsthetic quality. Similarity of purposive inspiration might have suggested this isolation of several books into one æsthetic group; but it is the continuity of material that really effects it. So the originating necessity becomes the admirable artistic virtue of isolation; it enables the series of Hardy's great novels to assume the air of a single work of art. Thereby each of these seven novels has a greatly enhanced value for the reader who can see its place as a component of the whole group; almost as much as each act of a play has more than its intrinsic significance through being part of the whole play.

This is evidently the place to speak briefly of Hardy's use of nature in his novels; briefly, because this quality has several times already received its full share of examination. Probably it is the most famous of all the easily distinguishable qualities in the novels. When Hardy's fiction took a turn disturbing to the conscience of the great English public, those who remained faithful, if a trifle dubious, would say, "But at least admire the descriptions!" And to do the objectors justice, they usually were ready to admire the descriptions. The thing first to be noticed here, however (it has already been mentioned), is that these descriptions are never detachable ornament. Even such elaborate accounts as those of Egdon Heath, and of the Vales of Blackmoor and Froom, are parts not only of the substance but of the action of the story. Nature, indeed, in Hardy's fiction is neither an abstraction nor a scenic setting, but a vast impassive organism, living her own immense life, multitudinous but obscurely unanimous; and the strict formality of the art could have no use for this enormous being unless it was able to bear some part in the fable, whose event becomes, therefore, an affair only partially human. There is wonderful sensitiveness to natural beauty and grandeur in the Wessex Novels; but there is a good deal more. There is the hard, practical, exact knowledge of nature's workings which shepherds and farm labourers must have. As an instance of this, and of the exhibition of nature actively par-

CHARACTERISTICS

ticipating in the story, the presages of the storm in *Far from the Madding Crowd* (Chapter XXXVI.) would do better than the celebrated descriptions just mentioned. Nature, in fact, holds the human action in solution; and this does more efficiently whatever can be done by using nature as a scenic setting—in the way, for instance, of spacing the action broadly in the open air.

Here also, in Hardy's use of nature, there is obvious limitation; in this case plainly deliberate. The novels never trespass outside Wessex. It would seem that this is a conscious result of that instinct for form with which this chapter has been chiefly concerned. For it cannot be questioned that this limitation of locality powerfully seconds the limitation of human material in causing that sense of admirable æsthetic isolation when we consider the Wessex Novels (or rather the best of them) as a whole; a body of work that stands singular and by itself. And besides giving this desirable sense of an art concentrated within strict boundaries, this limitation of locality is fortunate in another respect. Just as the human material, which the novels most successfully use, is a class of greater variety than any other well-defined section of society, and is moreover through all its varieties obviously suitable to the special kind of tragedy required by Hardy's genius; so also is it with Wessex, with the country in which the novels are imaginatively placed. Such changeable landscape is hardly to be found anywhere else in England; and yet there is a feeling of identity running through all the changes. In a single day you may walk through a mass of turbulent little hills, low but of good upstanding attitude, gashed into innumerable valleys, pockets of rich soil; through straggling upland hamlets, well known to the winds, and through compact, orderly, lowland villages, coloured with gardens and climbing flowers; through spaces of desolate brown heath, and through wide flat vales of almost oppressive fertility, vivid meadows that seem to shine against your eyes, watered with clear rivers full of fat trout and golden clotes; until you arrive at great stretches of smooth downland, and so come to a coast of abrupt grandeur. Through all this variety flows a certain simple nobility of design, which unifies it and prevents each kind from becoming paramount; the barren kind is not formidable, and the fertile is not too pretty. And both the variety and the underlying simplicity make it a country exactly fit for supplying Hardy's genius with the inspiration it required; unless I should say, Hardy's genius is exactly suited to the inspiration supplied by this countryside.

CHARACTERISTICS

Beyond noting this, however, criticism cannot have much to do with Wessex itself. Tours in Wiltshire and Dorsetshire are wisely undertaken, if their purpose is a view of those beautiful counties; they are curiously futile, if their purpose is to get somehow nearer to the art of the Wessex Novels. Wessex in the novels is simply a creature used for a special artistic purpose; apart from that purpose it has, artistically, no significance. The elaborate system of altering the place-names should be a sufficient hint of this. However much the actual Wessex may interest and delight, such feelings will not help us to enjoy Hardy, any more than a reading of Roman history or Saxo Grammaticus will add to the significance of Julius Cæsar or Hamlet. Still, explorations in Wessex guided by one of the several handbooks of Hardy geography are harmless entertainment; and if the handbook get lost, and the relation of Dorset to the novels' South Wessex be forgotten, they will become as philosophic as any other tours through admirable landscape. Otherwise the tourist will certainly be teased by conscious or unconscious perception that art is one thing and reality another; that, for instance, the charm of Casterbridge is certainly not to be found in the pleasant old town of Dorchester.

Hardy's limitations may possibly, in regard to

his human material—must certainly, in regard to his use of locality—be considered as varying expressions of his remarkable instinct for æsthetic form. But there is one other limitation to be discussed ; not dissimilar in nature to these others, but one that could never be taken or mistaken for an advantage. This is in regard to the style of his writing. I suppose no sane admirer of Hardy's work has ever gone the length of calling him a master of language. Language with him on the whole is an instrument—an efficient one, to be sure; but it is seldom an organism. The words, in the general texture of his work, are words used much as a scientist, scarcely as a poet, would use them. With the scientist, the value of words depends on their place in a sentence, their individual obedience to a general purport; with the poet, this logical value of words is compounded with an additional value, just as considerable, which is absolutely their own, quite apart from any sentence wherein they may be of use. And this additional value does not embarrass the other, but on the contrary gives it surprising potency; for the thought of a poet is not something that can be stated precisely in words, and there an end. It shades off all round from the precise into the indefinite and incommunicable, into what can only be suggested.

CHARACTERISTICS

He tries, therefore, to give his thought not only a logical statement in words, but also to infect his reader's mind with the vague aura surrounding his thought, by so organizing his logical words that their essential, hyper-logical value is noticeably and appropriately used. Such organizing of language will vehemently empower the logic beyond anything that can be effected by the mere instrumental use of language; but, most conspicuously, it gives words that challenging and exciting quality which they only have when they are used as things existing for themselves as well as for logic. I shall adopt here, and in later chapters, the terminology invented by Mr. Arthur Ransome. He divides the energy of words into "kinetic" and "potential," on an obvious analogy; "kinetic" being what I have roughly called their logical force, "potential" their exciting force. This admirable device, perhaps the most useful of recent additions to the apparatus of criticism, can scarcely be dispensed with in any nice examination of diction; it is especially useful in the case of a writer like Hardy.

All language (except perhaps in cookery books and the statement of geometrical problems) must be both kinetic and potential. The ordinary user of language, the man who uses words as an engine for the statement of precise thought, is consciously concerned only with their kinetic energy; but words inevitably carry with them, and he must unconsciously employ, their potential energy. The latter, however, in such use of words, is subdued and merged in the kinetic; it does not challenge the reader's admiration and delight; he is left to admire only the words' logical obedience. But the man who has really mastered language is one to whom the knowledge of how to write logically is but half the business; he consciously employs potential as well as kinetic; and the reader's pleasure in logical form is continually reinforced by some sudden liberation of a word's essential and characteristic energy. This kind of writing is almost wholly lacking in the great bulk of Hardy's prose. It is language used consciously only for its kinetic power; the potential is there, as it must be in all intelligent diction; but it is implicit, it is manifest only feebly and accidentally, for conscious intention is needed to make the exciting force of words tell. Yet there are occasional passages wherein the potential of words does find some exciting liberation in Hardy's prose. They are usually passages that evidently come out of long intense brooding on the appearance of the earth. Nature has assumed the quality of concealed personality; and the strong efforts to seize this into words seem to cause an unwonted illumination of the riches held in words themselves. The famous description of Egdon Heath, to which this chapter has already several times referred, is a very remarkable instance of this also.

But when we consider Hardy's use of dialect, we must at once perceive that, in this question of style, we are again dealing not so much with disability as with limitation. It is with his language as with his characters. When he is concerned with rusticity, of persons or of language, the surface of his work, however charming in itself, is always to be felt as the manifestation of inwardness; but in the case of his polite people and his polite language, he is so much concerned with keeping the surface polite that he gives us little else than surface. And unfortunately, novels must be written in polite language. But when we pass from the general texture of the narrative into a rustic conversation, the difference is amazing; just as amazing as the sudden change from the respectable prosing of Scott's polite style to the superb, glowing language of " Wandering Willie's Tale " in "Redgauntlet." It is a jump into another world; from a world in which words are merely honestly and faithfully logical, to one in which they are " Virtues and Powers," where they move charged with incalculable potentials, radiating that strange suggestiveness which is the poetic value of words. Let me give a specimen of the vivid, nervous, darting speech Hardy gives to his rustics; it is a merely typical case of their exquisite vain-glorying :

"I once hinted my mind to her on a few things, as nearly as a battered frame dared to do so to such a forward piece. You all know, neighbours, what a man I be, and how I come down with my powerful words when my pride is boiling wi' scarn?"

"We do, we do, Henery."

"So I said, 'Mistress Everdene, there's places empty, and there's gifted men willing; but the spite'—no, not the spite—I didn't say spite—'but the villainy of the contrari-kind,' I said (meaning womankind), 'keeps 'em out.' That wasn't too strong for her, say?"

"Passably well put."

"Yes; and I would have said it, had death and salvation overtook me for it. Such is my spirit when I have a mind."

"A true man, and proud as a lucifer."

. . . . . .

"A strange old piece, goodmen—whirled about from here to yonder, as if I were nothing! A little warped, too. But I have my depths; ha, and even my great depths! I might gird at a certain shepherd, brain to brain. But no—— Oh no!"

"A strange old piece, ye say!" interposed the maltster, in a querulous voice. "At the same time ye be no old man worth naming—no old man at all. Yer teeth baint half gone yet; and what's a old man's standing if so be his teeth baint gone? Weren't I stale in wedlock afore

CHARACTERISTICS

ye were out of arms? 'Tis a poor thing to be sixty, when there's people far past fourscore—a boast weak as water."

. . . . . .

"Weak as water! Yes," said Jan Coggan. "Malter, we feel ye to be a wonderful veteran man, and nobody can gainsay it."

"Nobody," said Joseph Poorgrass. "Ye be a very rare old spectacle, malter, and we all respect ye for that gift."

"Ay, and as a young man, when my senses were in prosperity, I was likewise liked by a good-few who knowed me," said the maltster.

This dialect is by no means an affair of laboured phonetic spelling; "scarn" and "baint" are but flavouring. It is fine English made out of dialect, rather than dialect itself; for successful art can no more be satisfied with reality of language than with reality of event: both must be improved and formed. Obviously, however, the material was excellent; a language full of potential vigour of a kind that is evidently more suited to Hardy's personal expression than the shyer kind with which polite or "literary" English is charged. So suited to him is it, that he seems unable to avoid animating it with the imaginative verve which only the potential of language can convey. The potential of polite language makes but little appeal to him; and the enthusiasm of thought, when this is the medium, goes therefore unexpressed. The difference between his narrative and his dialect style is the difference between substance and vitality, between mechanism and organism.[1]

In the following chapters Hardy's books will not be dealt with chronologically, but in a classification based on their artistic significance, as I see it. There is no particular virtue in chronological classification; it must be chiefly founded on order of publication, and this may be but loosely related to order of composition, and hardly at all related to order of conception. Who is to say how long an artist has been carrying the idea and the form of a work in his mind? Who can tell what unconscious characteristics of an earlier period will be precipitated when the work comes to be written down? The futility of chronological treatment is best seen in those artists whose chronology has been most carefully studied. Beethoven, for instance; there is little precision of real order when his works are put in time-order; there is continual transgression of chronology in style and idea, harking back and anticipation. Equally futile is it to expect that by arranging the works of a man whose chronology is speculative (Shakespeare, for in-

[1] The dialect is also more correct. For instance, it says "malter" and not "maltster," knowing very well that "maltster" properly means "she-malter." Hardy, of course, cannot be charged with this inaccuracy. It is one of the interesting, but not perhaps very important, mistakes that literary speech frequently makes.

CHARACTERISTICS

stance), in some series marked by apparent regular development, we have thereby arranged the works in order of composition. The mind and work of an artist do not develop with this easy regularity; it is the delusion of an age which instinctively regards progress as a sort of railway train. Consider, in the case of Hardy, the chronological order of his first six books: *Desperate Remedies, Under the Greenwood Tree, A Pair of Blue Eyes, Far from the Madding Crowd, The Hand of Ethelberta, The Return of the Native.* Not a very regular development there! Much better, surely, to arrange the books according to their own interrelationships, not neglecting chronology, but refusing its tyranny.

Nevertheless, it will be convenient to give in the following list the dates of Hardy's chief publications in England:

[1840. Thomas Hardy born at Upper Bockhampton, near Dorchester.]
1871. Desperate Remedies.
1872. Under the Greenwood Tree.
1873. A Pair of Blue Eyes.
1874. Far from the Madding Crowd.
1876. The Hand of Ethelberta (serially in 1875).
1878. The Return of the Native.
1880. The Trumpet-Major.
1881. A Laodicean.
1882. Two on a Tower.

THOMAS HARDY

1883. Romantic Adventures of a Milkmaid (*Graphic* Summer Number).
1886. The Mayor of Casterbridge.
1887. The Woodlanders.
1888. Wessex Tales.
1891. A Group of Noble Dames (serially, *Graphic* Christmas Number, 1890).
1891. Tess of the D'Urbervilles.
1894. Life's Little Ironies.
1896. Jude the Obscure (serially, in mangled form, in 1894–5, under titles "The Simpletons" and "Hearts Insurgent").
1897. The Well-Beloved (serially, as "The Pursuit of the Well-Beloved," in 1892).
1898. Wessex Poems.
1901. Poems of Past and Present.
1903. ⎫
1906. ⎬ The Dynasts, Parts I, II, and III.
1908. ⎭
1909. Time's Laughing-stocks.

III

MINOR NOVELS

DESPERATE REMEDIES : A PAIR OF BLUE EYES :
THE HAND OF ETHELBERTA : A LAODICEAN :
THE WELL-BELOVED

THERE is not much experiment perceptible in the progress of Hardy's fiction; though towards the end we shall find a definite change in the manner of his construction. But *Under the Greenwood Tree* is already the work of one who has got his material under perfect control; and this is the second novel in order of publication. And with the fourth in that order, *Far from the Madding Crowd*, published only three years after the appearance of his first book, his genius has reached full scope; for it may easily be maintained that his later fiction has done no more than equal this exquisite early thing. But there are a number of novels which, though not tentative, are of slight importance in a general consideration of Hardy's work. Several of these are, no doubt, relaxations from severer efforts; during the first dozen years of produc-

THOMAS HARDY

tion there is a quite regular alternation from large to slight design. This is very natural, for it means only that genius has been resting between its achievements. The talent is pretty much the same in all the novels; but in the slighter tales it works for its own sake. The genius, which so strongly controls the talent of the great novels, is here fitfully employed, and is certainly not in command. Merely talented work is often the most profitable holiday an artist of genius can take; his genius, one might say, finds the best encouragement for a fresh attempt in watching how its lieutenant works alone.

The power of consistently imagining human beings, with all their individual wills and desires, as special manifestations of a universal tendency, which has possession of everything in them except the assertions of self-consciousness; and the power of shaping forth this imagination in a rigorous human action: these two combined powers of conception and creation form the profound characteristic of Hardy's genius. These are the things, then, his novels of talent miss. They show an admirable skill for surface. They charm and they excite; but, except for a casual incident or two, when they are read they are done with. Talent in each has done its varying best; but that is not an effect of the story as a

MINOR NOVELS

whole, apart from its separable incidents, which is remembered for a great imaginative experience. On the whole, these novels of talent are not closely concerned with country folk; rusticity in them is used as a contrast to the main business. Their author, that is to say, only casually employs in them that kind of human material which his genius most easily works in, which enables him to symbolize in terms of concrete action his fundamental conception of the human state. And it is in these brief contrasting passages that we most easily find the Hardy of the greater novels. Perhaps it is worth noticing, too, that when it is talent, and not genius, that has the chief management of his fiction, he is ready to use the circumstances of his own experience; the profession of architecture is a principal ingredient in no less than three of these slighter novels: *Desperate Remedies*, *A Pair of Blue Eyes*, and *A Laodicean*. In spite of such great instances to the contrary as Goethe and Dante, those writers who, at their best, are conspicuous for imaginative rather than imitative power, generally use personal experience to supply the failure of inspiration.

Four of these lesser novels, published during the first ten years of Hardy's output, are chiefly considerable as studies, no doubt of great importance to the facility of subsequent work, in the exercise of two kinds of skill: the plotting out of a story, and the drawing of feminine character. *Desperate Remedies* is an affair of long, ingenious complications; too exclusively, as its preface now admits, of "mystery, entanglement, surprise, and moral obliquity." It is an exciting story, even though the excitements are somewhat deliberately devised; and the subordinate rustic comedy that centres in the "Three Tranters Inn" is of unmistakable quality, though perhaps it would hardly prepare us for *Under the Greenwood Tree*, which appeared a year later. Psychologically, the tale is of two women, the vehement Miss Aldclyffe and the gentle Cytherea; and their outlines, sometimes stiff rather than definite, sometimes shadowy rather than subtle, nevertheless suggest several characteristic heroines of the later novels, especially in their mingled impulse and reserve. But *Desperate Remedies* is chiefly a study in plot. *A Pair of Blue Eyes* has a less surprising plot, but a far more absorbing one, strictly devised to lead up to a climax, not of mystery discovered, but of quite admirable tragic irony. The two friendly disappointed rivals, each hastening down to forestall the other in an interview with the impressionable beloved, find that the train which is carrying them on their hopeful errand is also carrying the lady herself, but carrying her to her grave. The sudden turn from pathos to comedy, and from comedy to tragedy, betrays the master of plot—rather, it is formal mastery that has now arrived; plot is too narrow a word for the power this book shows of putting a complexity of affairs into the control of a single cogency. The talent is now ready for genius to use in a much larger and deeper scope of imagination; the following year, with *Far from the Madding Crowd*, sees it so used. Elfride, the indiscreet, impulsive heroine of *A Pair of Blue Eyes*, is a charming person, drawn with real subtlety, with lines of exact yet delicate stroke. She is not, indeed, to be compared with her immediate successor, Bathsheba Everdene; but the masterful drawing of Bathsheba seems to owe something to the practice Elfride provided in the way of figuring a creature of incalculable impulse whose personality is yet not fluid but definitely formed. This novel, too, contains some admirable rustics; notably William Worm, plagued with the noises in his head ("Fizz, fizz, fizz; 'tis frying o' fish from morning to night") and complaining against Providence ("Providence is a merciful man, and I have hoped He'd have found it out by this time, living so many years in a parson's family, too, as I have, but 'a don't seem to relieve me "). The adventure on the cliff-top is a very memorable incident; the dread of height has seldom gone into language with such small loss of its grisly force; the passage is a fine instance of the patient intensity of Hardy's writing on crucial occasions—deliberately, with almost perceptible labour, building up words into the exact shape of some formidable emotion. And yet, when all is said, *A Pair of Blue Eyes* is a slight book; slight, that is, compared with the novel which followed it. It is a well-ordered system of charming, pathetic, but unimportant occurrences; unimportant, because, when their system has rounded to its close, they have not managed to convey any general significance, any suggestion of life as a whole underlying individual appearance.

The Hand of Ethelberta does not call for much comment. Ethelberta herself is a bustling, managing, rapid-minded, unscrupulous, rather lovable wench; but her invasion of high society is a tiresome business long before it is finished. The story is so drawn out that it is almost rambling; and it is difficult to be interested in its gentry. The opening is good, so good that it carries one a considerable way into the tale before lassitude becomes noticeable; but the reader will scarcely find in the succeeding forty-six chapters anything as taking as the first, with its conversation of milkman and hostler, and Ethelberta's chase of the duck-hawk. Hardy has an excellent knack of setting a narrative going. It is very noticeable again in *A Laodicean;* the baptism scene is not easily resisted. Neither is the rest of the story; the plot is managed with delightful skill. But the novel is obviously meant to satisfy certain well-known preferences of public taste; and, in spite of its cunning plot and the amiable (but not very distinguished) character of Paula, there is perhaps less of the Hardy that matters in *A Laodicean* than in any other of his books. *The Romantic Adventures of a Milkmaid*, though it has not, apparently, been thought worthy of republication,[1] is much more genuinely character-istic. The romantic apparatus is, to be sure, somewhat preposterous; but it is quite plea-santly preposterous, and turns to a pretty irony. The fascinated milkmaid, with her childish heart and her patient endurance of disappointment, is fantastic, but finely imagined; and her lover the limeburner, who "suffered horseflesh" on her account, is not unlike the reddleman of *The Return of the Native,* for the absorption of his trade into his personality. The descriptive

---

[1] This novelette appeared in the *Graphic* Summer Number of 1883; there has been an American reprint—whether authorized or not I do not know.

passages are sketchily done; but they are curiously effective; notably one at the beginning, only a few lines long, of the milkmaid walking through the soaking fog of early morning, and avoiding, for her bonnet's sake, the shower-baths of the trees: the colour and smell and quiet of early morning in the valley are fixed in those few lines. The landscape of the tale seems to be a study for the elaborately finished landscape of the dairy-farming part in *Tess of the D'Urbervilles*.

The novels this chapter has been so far considering have been removed, for convenience of discussion, from the main series of Hardy's work, because they are slight in purpose rather than in material; the greater novels do not use an altogether different substance, but contract it into a defined range of society, and transfigure it by a profound purpose. From these greater and these lesser novels alike, *The Well-Beloved* stands clearly apart; the slightness here is in the material. It is the only novel of Hardy's in which the symbolic purpose, instead of appearing as the result of a certain ordering of the material, appears, on the contrary, to be drawing the material somewhat unwillingly after it. Our feeling, when we read this novel, is not, Here is a set of circumstances of which the resultant effect is so-and-so; but, Here is an effect which may, for the convenience of narrative, be supposed as occurring in such-and-such a set of circumstances. In a word, *The Well-Beloved* is frankly fantastic: it must be read just for the sake of its idea, not for the verisimilitude of its substance. It has already been remarked, that Hardy's heroines commonly prove decidedly disastrous to their lovers; this is as obvious in *A Pair of Blue Eyes* as in most of the greater novels. In the minds of those writers who have held to the ruinous power of love and women, the usual corollary—it is a sort of revenge—is the notion of the eternal inadequacy of women to the love they inspire; not only misogynists believe it, but idealists like William Morris, whose type of feminine perfection says:

> " I am true, but my face is a snare;
> Soft and deep are my eyes,
> And they seem for men's beguiling
> Fulfilled with the dreams of the wise.
> Kind are my lips, and they look
> As though my soul had learned
> Deep things I have never heard of."

This notion is very well for philosophers and lyrical poets, but it does not do for dramatists (and novelists are a kind of dramatists), for their business is an unequivocal dealing with objective life, invigorated but unperturbed by subjective, notional life. Hardy, therefore, generally avoids drawing woman as a "snare" in Morris' sense; *The Well-Beloved* stands by itself in that it was written entirely to elaborate this notion. Its singularity in the series of his works makes it remarkable; but it is not a novel of any very notable success.

The amorous sentiment which possesses the central character is, however, a very interesting practical variety of the Platonic theory of love. In modern literature, the theory of ideal love—of love, namely, which is something more than a refinement of sexual desire—works out into two kinds of practice, directly opposed. In both, man is dominated by the desire for a transcendental perfection. Dante is the great instance of the one kind. With him the desire can only be aroused from its sleep in man's heart by vision of one who is not only a credible image of perfection, but who, for the man concerned, actually *is* the eternal perfection temporally embodied. Once roused, therefore, the desire can never change its object without sinning against love; but also, the desire can never be satisfied unless in the beatific vision; since, though roused among temporal affairs, it is a desire for one eternal thing. But in the other and much commoner variety of Platonic love—for it takes a Dante to live the experience of "La Vita Nuova" and the imagination of

"Paradiso"—the desire always falls short of satisfaction for a very different reason. It is for ever being roused, not by the image but by the mere hope of perfection; instead of being excited once and for all into adoration of one single person, it is always restlessly venturing forth and alighting like a radiation on her who chances to be in its way. The women whom the desire illuminates are not even its passing embodiments; they are simply the objects which, by being illumined, make the illumination visible, just as sunlight is invisible until it meets with opacity. So it is only the gleaming of his own desire that the lover worships; each amour ends in the desire being once more disappointed of perfection, as soon as the lover is able to distinguish the woman underneath the dazzling transfiguration he himself has caused; the ideal love becomes a ceaseless irony. But in the best known instances of it the process has not stopped here. In Shelley, it turns to a passionate belief in a real beauty which, though itself elusive, magnetizes the whole matter of the world; in Cavalcanti and Leopardi it turns, on the contrary, to an impotent wrath with love, and no doubt this also underlies the sentiment of the famous "odi et amo" of Catullus, most modern of antique poets. In Hardy's *The Well-Beloved*, the result of ironical Platonic love falls whimsically between these two extremes. The hero is a sculptor, and his search for beauty in art is but another expression of the desire for the ideal which keeps his changeable heart unchangeably enamoured. And of what it is that happens to him when he falls in love he can only say, with Catullus, "nescio sed . . . excrucior!" But he does not go to any height in either consequence of his unwillingly ironic Platonism; neither in his worship of beauty nor in his wrath with love. He is a mediocre person, and his tragedy is merely that he becomes ridiculous, even to himself; for the chief events in his medley of amours are his successive affairs, at twenty-year-intervals, with a woman, her daughter, and her granddaughter. This might have made a pleasant comedy of ironic Platonism; but the book is fatally slight in its psychology. We know nothing of the hero except his unlucky trick of falling in and falling out of love, always expecting his ideal and never finding anything like it; and this trick of his is not made really credible —it must simply be accepted for the purposes of narrative. Nevertheless, the novel is an interesting attempt; and, if somewhat unconvincing in its *naïveté*, it is at any rate a clear and straightforward account of a psychological condition which has hitherto gone into literature chiefly in the cipher of subjective lyrics. The book pleasantly reminds us, too, of what the poets usually forget, namely, that to be the temporary object of a man's idealizing love does not make a woman a nonentity; she herself may at the same time be similarly idealizing the man, and be as ready as he is to own herself disappointed when the reality of the beloved "grins through"—as painters say of the grain of wood—the glamour of her love.

IV

ANNEXES

WESSEX TALES : LIFE'S LITTLE IRONIES : A GROUP OF NOBLE DAMES : A FEW CRUSTED CHARACTERS : THE TRUMPET-MAJOR : TWO ON A TOWER : UNDER THE GREENWOOD TREE

WORDSWORTH, in a famous preface, likened the intention of his proposed great trilogy of poems to the body of a Gothic church, round which, he said, the best of his shorter poems would be found to attach themselves like side-chapels and oratories. The simile is not inappropriate to the writings of Thomas Hardy, if we leave out the comparatively unimportant books discussed in the last chapter. For it is very easy to look at Hardy's work as a whole. Its main bulk is quarried out of one stratum of human substance; there is an evident idiosyncrasy of design running through all its various structures; and, from *Under the Greenwood Tree* and *Far from the Madding Crowd* to *The Dynasts* and *Time's Laughing-stocks*, the whole matter of his writing is the vehicle of one con-

ANNEXES

tinuous purposive emotion, all its imageries conform to one chief obedience, a certain constant sentiment or disposition, in the mind of their inventor, "to Man and Nature and to Human Life." In the great building, which fancy easily sees Hardy's several books uniting to shape, the pillared nave would be the series of the six principal novels; unless the two last of them should be seen as transepts, since each of these is large enough to stand somewhat by itself. *Under the Greenwood Tree* might be the porch or ante-chapel; and certainly *The Dynasts* must be the quire, a place, as sometimes happens, of loftier proportions, more intricate carving and more varied material than the nave through which it is approached. This is the main building; but round about, though not separate, supporting but not intimately concerned in the chief composition of the building, there are, like side-chapels and miscellaneous recesses, the poems, the short stories, and two other novels. It is with such annexes to the main building that this chapter will deal; leaving, however, the poems for a later chapter. This proposed architectural image of Hardy's work as a whole is useful for the kind of completeness and wholeness of general design which it suggests—one main continuity of expression surrounded by subordinate yet not detached varieties; but the simile, to be sure, must not be pressed too closely. The spirit of the building which fantasy thus forms of Hardy's tales and poems is far enough from anything ecclesiastic; it is, no question, a spirit of large and grave dignity, but also it is a spirit of rough, sensuous comedy, and of a scepticism that refuses everything but the general tragic fatality of existence.

First, then, for the short stories. They may be said, broadly, to decorate, rather than to add to the general significance of Hardy's artistic structure. This is hardly what would be expected, if one came to these short stories after reading the best of the novels. For in Hardy's hands, fiction has done, in the scale of the novel, what previously it could only do with certainty and ease in the scale of the short story; the power of making a human action render, with astonishing impressiveness, and by means of a most exact formality, some metaphysic of existence is clear in Hawthorne's tales. But, splendid as several of his novels are, this power is only diluted when Hawthorne works to the scale of the novel. With Hardy it is the other way round; to exercise this power, his fiction requires expatiation rather than concentration. But, though his short stories are a decoration for his main literary structure, they are entirely appropriate decoration. They give us, in varying forms and manners, his characteristic vision of life; what we miss in them is the subtle declaration of what that vision profoundly *means* to his inmost emotion. If they do not add much power to the effect of his writings as a whole, they nevertheless perfectly fit in with it. Consider, as types of the rest, the two stories which are probably the best known of these shorter pieces: *The Three Strangers* and *The Withered Arm*. Here, concentrated into terse and vivid drama, is precisely the same vision of life as that which is wrought into larger and more significant form in the novels. We are set to watch a process of life which goes as inevitably and as involuntarily as a process of chemistry. Certain elements appear, variously combined, and distributed through the indifferent mass of surrounding humanity—the " heap of flesh," as he somewhere calls it. But however compounded and scattered, these elements are irresistibly moved to work towards one another by strong affinity; and the human molecules in which they are ingredients are dragged along with them, until the elemental affinity is satisfied, in a sudden flashing moment of disintegration and re-compounding. The new compound into which these elements arrange themselves is, in the short stories, a tragical or ironical situation; with this *solid* result the experiment in the chemistry of life stops. But in the great novels a nicer investigation is added; there is attempt to catch and estimate the fine escape of insensible vapour which accompanies the process; there, in a word, the result is not merely the solid tangible one of human situation, but is also a significance, intellectual and spiritual.

The Three Strangers is perhaps the best instance of sheer situation in the short stories. The controlled fear of the fugitive condemned criminal, the hangman's cheerful pride in his duty (the hangman is an admirable creature), and the amazed distress of the fugitive's brother —these are the elements that work towards each other. The rustic christening feast, which holds them like a solution, suddenly precipitates them compounded into a tragical situation; the compound, however, is not stable; it breaks up and goes once more into solution. But the experiment was exciting. In *The Withered Arm*, it is no fleeting compound of tragedy that results, but one as stable as it is grim. The slow and formidable process of this tale has for its most urgent activity a dreadful superstition, which irresistibly drives forward the involuntary blasting hatred of the cast-off mistress, the misery of the barren wife changed from beauty

ANNEXES

to strange deformity, the husband's disgust with her childlessness and mysterious malady, and his remorse for the bastard he had abandoned, until at last all these movements rush together into a blazing instant and settle in tragic equilibrium. There is a good deal of variety in Hardy's short stories; but the two just mentioned, thus chemically imaged, may serve as types of the manner and substance of the rest. The others are more often ironical than tragical in result. *The Distracted Preacher* is possibly the finest of these experiments in irony. Most of it is an excellent comedy of the humours of smuggling; and it is especially notable for its brilliant picture of the smuggling widow, Mrs. Lizzy Newberry. The irony is kept for the last paragraph. For this adventurous, high-spirited, contriving, vigorous young woman falls in love with a preaching nincompoop, and gives up her racy life to go with him through the duties of his dismal religion. She ought soon to weary of him; but what happens is only too credible: the admirable wench becomes subdued to the religion of her pithless husband, and gets in the end to writing tracts wherein her former masterful qualities are shown up as horrible instances of unregenerate nature. There is no need to go through all the other stories. Memorable in them are the two ambitious curates so plagued by their rapscallion father that they virtually murder him ; the man who endangers a woman's happiness not by betraying her, but by seeking to repair her supposed ruin in the conventional fashion ; the effect of sea-sickness in revealing unsuspected blood-relationship ; fascination by music in *The Fiddler of the Reels* and by correspondence in *On the Western Circuit*. But besides the two miscellanies of detached short stories, there are also two sets of several tales organized together by the supposed continuous occasion of their telling ; and something must be said of these.

The method of the " Decameron " and the "Canterbury Tales" has had many imitators; and it is a remarkably pleasing kind of narrative. It is a method which not only embraces the art of story-telling itself, but also, and very agreeably, the first origins of the art, its primary function in society. When several companions come together and fall to amusing themselves with exchange of anecdotes, it is the occasion as well as the stories which they enjoy. So, when Boccaccio's method of giving stories a setting is skilfully employed, to the quality of the stories themselves is added a certain intimate pleasure derived from the supposed personality of each narrator, and from his imaginary friendship with the other narrators ;

ANNEXES

and there is besides the pleasure of feeling the batch of stories coalescing into a single unity of effect—the effect, namely, of the whole occasion, with its atmosphere and psychology. For in a group of men who have become sufficiently companionable to tell each other stories, there will be formed a communal genial spirit which is a good deal more than the sum of their separate persons. It is the spirit of the occasion, unique but transient, which electrifies its members, so that they enjoy what happens there for more than its own sake. This is the spirit which must first be invented as the region, so to say, for this organized kind of story-telling; but its nature and intensity must chiefly be exhibited in the various stories themselves.

Evidently, this is work only for a talent of great formative power; but that is as much as to say it is work well suited to Hardy's talent. His two experiments in this kind of work are not specially ambitious, but they are finely successful, and they follow the three great instances of organized story-telling in making the occasion, which the tales create, itself the expression of something further—though, certainly, not of anything comparable with the profound zest for life behind the " Decameron," or the immense sympathy with actual mankind of the " Canterbury Tales," or the aspiration for an ideal mankind of "The Earthly Paradise."

A Group of Noble Dames supposes for its occasion a meeting of a Wessex Field and Antiquarian Club, " of an inclusive and intersocial character." Its members belong to a placid community which is little disturbed by the spirit of the time, one wherein "honest squires, tradesmen, parsons, clerks, and people still praise the Lord with one voice for His best of all possible worlds." The stories told in this society are ironic and unconscious criticisms of the world thus envisaged by religious and mental complacency; in the tales put into the mouths of the unsuspecting narrators, the world of respectable optimism suffers, without knowing anything about it, a considerable invasion from Hardy's world of tragic fatalism. The usual proceedings of the club for some reason fall through; and, that the meeting may not be wasted, the clubmen conclude to tell each other stories drawn from the personal history of the county: the tales, indeed, are really based on oral traditions of well-known Wessex families. As might be expected from a male gathering, an understanding is formed that the stories must all deal with the fortunes and characters of women; and it seems that Wessex county history affords plenty of material, at any rate, for

ANNEXES

such narrative. *A Group of Noble Dames* is a wonderful series of feminine characters, vividly and subtly imagined. The book might be taken as an epitome of Hardy's feminine psychology. These "noble dames" are as ready to obey fantasy altogether in some things as to endure the sternest rigours of duty in others. There is something inevitable in their caprice; indeed, it is not properly caprice, but action that proceeds directly from the springs of emotion, without passing through the formulation and questioning of reason. It is, perhaps, more than anything else, this power of drawing inevitable caprice that makes Hardy one of the greatest inventors or describers of feminine character. One sees very clearly, too, in this book, how valuable this characteristic conception of female psychology is to Hardy's art; in its symbolic purpose, one of the most useful qualities it has. For this womanly caprice, with all its tragical result, becomes at last the very type of the impersonal, primal impulse of existence, driving forward all its varying forms of embodiment, profoundly working even within their own natures to force them onward in the great fatal movement of the world, all irrespective of their conscious desires. As for the stories themselves, they are concise and shapely pieces of narrative, whether their action be as elaborate as the first, with its complexity of characters and purposes, or, like the tale of the girl who fulfilled a jest of her girlhood and married her three suitors one after the other, as simple in construction as Boccaccio's tales. But it is the women themselves that we most willingly remember; such figures as the girl who infected herself with small-pox to escape the match proposed for her, but afterwards used the infection to test the qualities of her rival lovers; or the pitiful figure of the wife infatuated with the statue of her first lover, and fiendishly cured by her husband. The stories are not suited with any special care to their supposed narrators, though there is no incongruity of manner. The conversational intervals between the stories are briefly sketched; but they are enough to produce the quiet irony of the whole —these comfortable representatives of a world satisfied with unexamined formulæ, telling each other tragical tales which reveal, though they never suspect it, the reality of life's processes as something by no means to be contained in easy-going formulæ.

A Few Crusted Characters is the not very felicitous name of the other set of organized tales. It is smaller in scope and slighter in intention; but it is a little masterpiece. A man returns after a long absence to his native village, and for the final stage of his journey he

ANNEXES

takes the carrier's van from the market-town. He asks the other passengers for information about the people he had known in his youth; and his inquiries lead very naturally to a series of anecdotes concerning typical village characters. The whole business fits in perfectly with the occasion; the exile's return is realized with a sort of accumulative delicacy—the more delicately for the contrasting mood of vigorous rustic joking which pervades the stories, and underneath which the exile's return to the familiar sensations of his boyhood quietly progresses. And it is much more than this; if anyone wished to get, in the course of an hour or so, a pretty clear understanding of the whole spirit of rural England, of the quality of its life and manners, this exquisite little work would be the thing for him. Nothing could be more perfectly English; and what that epithet essentially means is a thing not easy to come by nowadays in life or in art. It is not a profound piece of literature. It consists chiefly of simple, not to say elementary, humour, as rough and as vigorous as a morris dance, though there is a touch of queer character here and there, and some superstition in it, and one fairly elaborate tragedy, containing a fine figure of relentless vengeance. But it is all a thing of admirable, unforced, kindly art. The persons, like the jokes, have the air of belonging to the common stock of humanity; the persons that will always be in the world, whatever other varieties of mankind may come and pass, and the jokes that will always be told, let invention do what it can. And yet here both persons and jokes are all entirely individual and unique; just what they are in these stories, they will never be, and have never been, anywhere else. The stories also have the advantage of being wholly written in that splendid language, charged with strength and fire, which Hardy has contrived out of the west-country dialect.

The Trumpet-Major and Robert his Brother is filled with a very similar spirit. What was said of a well-known play, might be said of this novel: "it seems written to make the reader happy." Pathos is in it, and even some approach to tragedy; but there is an excellent sweet temper presiding over the manner of the whole tale; and to read it is to live for a while in an English country village of the old style. The writing is decidedly more vivid and alive than in most of Hardy's novels; the racy dialect of the conversations seems to have infected the language of the whole narrative. It is full of fine energy, rich with gaiety and whimsical humour, running off into headlong catalogues of imagery, as if the words enjoyed their existence. The dialogue is full of epithetical vigour ("My scram blue-vinnied gallicrow of an uncle," for instance); and both dialogue and narrative continually discharge sharp, terse sentences of keen description, such as this of an old man's eyesight: "My sight is so gone off lately that things, one and all, be but a November mist to me"; or this, of a ship hull-down: "She was now no more than a dead fly's wing on a sheet of spider's web." It is one of those books that seem to make us live with purged senses; nothing escapes us. As we watch the troopers watering their horses, the whole charm of a summer early morning comes into us; and as we hear the sailor discoursing on Trafalgar, his words are accompanied by a softly-hummed melody—Anne unconsciously singing to herself for joy that her lover is safe (before she learns that his safety means his treachery to her love). Indeed, the book is so full of gusto that it frequently runs over into a delightful superfluity of description, which certainly no one would wish away; there is no resisting the zestful energy of the great house-cleaning, nor the preparations for the wedding feast, nor the relishing account of Casterbridge beer. *The Trumpet-Major* can hardly be called an historical novel; but it is an admirable realization of rural England in Napoleonic times; all nerves and hatred of Frenchmen underneath the placid habit of her existence, ready to break out into a wild scurry of mingled effort and fear when the bogy of invasion becomes suddenly insupportable, and as ready to fall back again into quiet ways. The story is a slight one; scarcely more than the distresses of a girl who, endeavouring to control her love and give it to the more worthy of her suitors, cannot do anything but love the less worthy. It ends happily for her, and for the genial shiftless sailor; but the soldier, an excellent fellow, must go off content with his steadfast honour as its own reward. The girl is a charming study; and her gentle bewilderment with a life which, she is sure, ought to be tranquil and simple, but persists in being disturbing and complex, is a pleasing counterpart to more tragical figures. The miller, and the widow, and some of the minor persons (like the corporal who delights to show off his ancient injuries), have, as the persons of the *Crusted Characters* have, that air of belonging to the common stock of humanity, which only a great writer can give with delight instead of tedium; but Festus Derriman, though a tolerable figure of fun, is rather too obviously the *miles gloriosus* of convention.

In our architectural image of Hardy's work as a whole, *Two on a Tower* was paired with *The*

ANNEXES

Trumpet-Major, the two books being, in size, the principal annexes to the main building. But the two can only be put together by reason of the important, and, as it were, mutually balancing position they hold among the other side-structures—short stories and poems—grouped about the loftier central portion of the whole design, the great novels and *The Dynasts*. Than *Two on a Tower* and *The Trumpet-Major*, no two novels by the same author could be more different, in spirit and in form. The eager gaiety which works so deliciously throughout the latter has given place, along with the abundant happy descriptiveness, to a graver spirit and a stricter form. This is a book whose beauty owes nothing to decoration. The lives of its composition are ordered with severe economy; nothing distracts from the poignant tragedy of the central theme. But the whole effect is one of extraordinary beauty. The book is pervaded by an exquisite melancholy, the melancholy which "dwells with Beauty—Beauty that must die." Its story goes through some wonderful flights of joyous rapture; but the joy is one "whose hand is ever at his lips, Bidding adieu." The deserted fine lady who pours out all her stores of passionate love on the youthful astronomer; her momentary terrible jealousies of his science; the relentless drift of their destiny, at first by external embarrassment making their private intimacy the sweeter, but at last dividing them; her desperate marriage with the bishop; her lover's return, still a youth, while she has aged; the agony of unlooked-for joy which kills her—this is a theme which, for sheer beauty of drama and character, Hardy has scarcely equalled anywhere else. Perhaps it is only because the book stands somewhat apart from the main series of the novels, and can have but little share in their advantage of a great common intention, wherein each one seems to shoulder up the other—perhaps it is only because of this separation, that *Two on a Tower* will hardly be reckoned one of its author's most significant performances. But I do not think this is really so; I think the book, for all the beauty of its spirit and the shapeliness of its design, does really stand, not only apart from, but below the great novels. Life, certainly, has been exquisitely formed to art in this story; but yet the artistic formation of life can go deeper than it does here; this novel is not a perfect satisfaction of formative desire. Its passionate action does not symbolize an inner formation of some large intellectual and ethical apprehension of life's whole affairs; not, at any rate, with anything like the cogency and easy certainty which give *The Mayor of Casterbridge* and *Tess of the D'Urbervilles* their title to greatness. There is some admirable comedy in the book, notably the scene in which the parson tries to persuade the quire to sing from tonic sol-fa ; but the closeness of the form does not leave much place for interludes of rustic dialogue, and the comedy comes in briefly, for the most part in single speeches rather than in scenes, the finest of these speeches being Haymoss Fry's history of Pa'son St. Cleeve's career, his headstrong marriage, his disgust with his profession of curing " twopenny souls," and his death in a nor'-west thunderstorm, " it being said—hee-hee !—that Master God was in tantrums wi'en for leaving his service." The novel has been humorously accused of irreverence to the Established Church on account of the character of the bishop. Bishops, perhaps, are not quite so sacrosanct nowadays as they used to be ; we are ready to believe that they may be more human than the expensive suits of ecclesiastical clothes for which Trollope's novels were so admired. And, anyway, this bishop, as Hardy pleasantly remarks in his preface, " is every inch a gentleman."

Under the Greenwood Tree was published just ten years before *Two on a Tower;* and it was the second book of Hardy's to appear. But already it announces the construction of the great series of novels of rural life to which his fame as a novelist is most firmly attached. That construction, as we have seen, was to divagate from its main direction of purpose into various subordinate expressions: but, during a period of twenty-four years following the issue of *Under the Greenwood Tree*, the great purpose is steadily built up, flanked by work of lower stature supported decoratively round it, into the lofty central body of structure—*Far from the Madding Crowd*, *The Return of the Native*, *The Mayor of Casterbridge*, *The Woodlanders*, *Tess of the D'Urbervilles*, and *Jude the Obscure;* a continual height of achievement, like the roof of a nave. Seven years later, *The Dynasts* begins to carry the central purpose still further, and at a higher pitch; by no means a summation of the rest in another form, but rather the final justification of the whole composition, the towering acme of the complete design, a roomy, elaborate bulk of structure to which all the preceding series of novels leads up, as nave leads to quire. The interval, before the immense process of this addition was made public, saw the appearance, as if in preparation for it, of two books, decorative annexes to the main body of prose, composed in the richer formality of verse; and the style of the building thus passes easily into the intricate complex workmanship of *The Dynasts*. The whole building, we may now

ANNEXES

suppose, is complete; anything added to it will be likely to decorate (as *Time's Laughing Stocks* did) its great structure of artistic purpose, rather than to carry the main design forward.

That design—an unconscious design, it need hardly be said, since it is really an exceptionally clear unifying characteristic working itself out, through several books, into complete expression—that design, now that we have the whole imposing edifice finished, is seen to be evidently beginning in *Under the Greenwood Tree*. The book is plainly in one line with the series of the principal novels; but it is, as plainly, a book that does not reach the tall level of its successors. It is, indeed, the porch through which one enters directly into the main body of Hardy's work, to see the whole length of the building stretching beyond. There is no large construction of narrative in this novel; we may regard it as a preliminary statement of the kind of material and, still more, the kind of spirit, which are to be more greatly and more elaborately used later. But it would be a strange mistake in judgment to value *Under the Greenwood Tree* only as the porch to the rest, and not for its own separate, and exquisite, sake. The rustic love of life, finely coloured by the rustic stoical acceptance of life's evils, is realized in this story with more profundity, perhaps, than might be expected from the even good-nature of it all. The characters do not do much, but they admirably live; the figures of the Mellstock quire, moving with deliberate humour through the scenes of this naïve comedy, obviously come from a hand that has gained a notable plastic mastery over the human substance. And few books take their readers into closer friendship with the earth. The author's genius has nothing more to learn in the way of controlling the skill of the talent submitted to it; the powers here employed need only a deeper intellectual adventurousness in the invention of theme, to become altogether adequate to the great work soon to be required of them.

V

DRAMATIC FORM

FAR FROM THE MADDING CROWD: THE RETURN OF THE NATIVE: THE MAYOR OF CASTERBRIDGE: THE WOODLANDERS

". . . It was one of those sequestered spots outside the gates of the world where may usually be found more meditation than action, and more listlessness than meditation; where reasoning proceeds on narrow premisses, and results in inferences wildly imaginative; yet where, from time to time, dramas of a grandeur and unity truly Sophoclean are enacted in the real, by virtue of the concentrated passions and closely-knit interdependence of the lives therein."

This sentence, from *The Woodlanders*, might very well be taken as a brief declaration of the conditions which Hardy's most considerable fiction has chosen for its governance; which, therefore, we must recognize if we are to appreciate it properly. We are not bound to believe that in Wessex Sophoclean dramas actually do occur "in the real"; Hardy, like most great artists, is probably too much absorbed in his art to perceive clearly the profound modification of reality which it involves; his instinct, no doubt, is to see reality as it appears in his writings—as something, namely, which puts forth into sensible expression his own peculiar convictions. But this instinct is formative; what it sees, it makes; and substance thus forged to shapely significance, though it is entirely natural to human desires, is certainly not natural to raw objective event. What, however, the latter part of the sentence quoted may truly mean, after allowing for the too generous assertion of an artist in love with his medium, is that "dramas of a grandeur and unity truly Sophoclean" may be *credibly* imagined in the substance proposed; without any violent or noticeable manipulation, this Wessex life will obey plastic desires, and pass easily, inevitably, into a formal embodiment of significance—in a word, into tragedy. It is for the sake of unity and grandeur, then, that Hardy's fiction works in the conditions this substance imposes; for unity, the complete achievement of form, and grandeur, the achievement of significance. But these two things are not distinctly separable one from another; they are, indeed, at bottom one thing only; for what is significance in art but the *formation*, intellectual or emotional, of some ultimate relationship—the casting of formal control as far as conception can reach? Unity, however, is the first and obvious artistic result of choosing a material so isolated from the rest of humanity, as the life that goes on in these " sequestered spots outside the gates of the world." For the artist who desires, as all great artists must, to do work of the strict and triumphant formality which we call unity, naturally looks for some kind of human substance which has already in itself a certain separateness from the generality of life; the experiment of extracting from some special instance a universal symbol requires first of all, like every other experiment, boundary and enclosure. It was for this reason that the old dramatists delighted in kings and heroes; not primarily because they were signal types of life, though that was an important secondary reason, but because in them, by their accidental position, the complete isolation required by art is already half accomplished. And for just the same reason Hardy chooses, for the material of his art, life sequestered and rural. Even when the scene supposes a biggish county town, like Dorchester in *The Mayor of Casterbridge*, he is at pains to emphasize the peculiar separateness of its life from the main community. No general significance is possible in a work of art without continual submission, through the whole of it, to a single purport—without, that is to say, formal unity; and formal unity is impossible without thorough isolation of the substance. So we have the apparent paradox, that an art of general significance is most likely to result when it chooses a substance obviously removed from the general activity of the world.

But the sequestered humanity with which Hardy treats in his greatest novels is further likely to yield artistic unity and significance for very important secondary reasons. One is, as he himself points out, "the closely-knit interdependence of the lives therein." There needs no elaborate artifice to create in such a life the human complex, sensitive through the whole to whatever affects its parts, which is the necessary instrument of drama. With only a slight intensifying of actual conditions, the personalities in Hardy's fiction are combined into systems of singularly intimate linkages. The communal life of these villages results in the closest interpenetration of influence and accident; and plainly this means that the most perfect unity may preside over a very complicated action. But this life, besides compelling its persons to fit closely in with one another, is also one of gradual and roomy processes, and its deliberate existence fosters deliberate individual character. Passion strikes

DRAMATIC FORM

deep and grows large; moreover, its dominance is little embarrassed by reasoned analysis. Reasoning, indeed, will here incorporate the desires of passion as readily as intellectual premisses, and cares nothing to distinguish the two compulsions; so that the simple, unhesitating faithfulness of Diggory Venn is as easily credible as the consuming frenzy of Farmer Boldwood. It is a life, too, which impregnates its persons deeply with the impersonal common vigours of the earth. Not only those are dyed by their surrounding circumstance of nature, who willingly know themselves immersed therein, like Giles Winterborne, Gabriel Oak, and Marty South; but those also who rebel against nature's possessing of them, like Eustacia, Wildeve, and Bathsheba, have, will they nill they, the stain of it in the tissues of their characters. And sometimes this immersion of personality in the larger surrounding life of nature is more acutely felt by the reader when it appears, not consciously known and profoundly delighted in, but in those who, for all their rebellion, do not perceive how completely they are dipt; there is an exquisitely subtle hint at this in the signals used by Eustacia and Wildeve—a stone thrown into a pool to sound like a hop-frog, a moth put through the chink of a window into a lighted room.

THOMAS HARDY

Now these latter conditions of the material substance Hardy's fiction has chosen, are evidently just those suited to that kind of "sightless substance"—that species of tragic significance—which his art aims at evoking. Characters who are without the protective weakness of analytic introspection, and readily give themselves to the urgency of passion, whether slow or violent, are moved to intensely personal effort by that which is the main impersonal motive force of universal vitality, which, indeed, will either gain its ends without troubling about the conscious wishes wherein it is embodied, or will destroy its vehicle in striving for them. Such characters simultaneously become helpless portions of life's impersonal, ruthless force, and thereby become also creatures of the fiercest personal experience. Moreover, there strongly flows through these characters a vigour still further removed from consciousness, the elemental vigour of the earth; of this their passion is but the human variety. In an art, then, which has such characters for its conspicuous figures, the unity formed in each particular human complex will be the general significance of *personality for ever moved to assert itself against the implacable, impersonal drift of things*—gaining thereby not the desired alteration of the unalterable, but simply a keener consciousness of human destiny; which, how-

DRAMATIC FORM

ever, is not an inconsiderable gain. The complete formation of this "sightless substance," in parallel with the material substance, is the grand quality of Hardy's characteristic fiction.

Of the six great novels which form the main building, in our architectural image, of Hardy's fiction, the two which were latest in publication show a marked difference from the others in their form. Roughly, but conveniently, the earlier books may be called dramatic, the two later epic, in form. The difference is chiefly in degree of complexity; but it is enough to put *Tess of the D'Urbervilles* and *Jude the Obscure* distinctly apart from the others. In the four earlier novels, the action is a woven intricacy of many curving and recurring lines, carrying the threaded lives of several persons through a single complicated pattern of destiny; for as the interest of the story concerns not one character, but several—a group, as a rule, of four contrasted personalities—its process is not a simple forward motion, but a system of vital currents ramified to and fro, the whole elaborate event obeying one general trend. They are polyphony, these four novels; whereas the two later books are great pieces of plain-song, each concerned with one human theme, which goes forward in unswerving continuity, not part of a broad stream of counterpoint, but accompanied by tones that follow it in unison. The difference between the two sets of novels is the difference between a history of an individual, and a history of the relationship in a group of individuals; and from this thematic difference, formal difference naturally follows. But *The Mayor of Casterbridge*, while clearly belonging, as regards its form, to the dramatic set, is in theme a partial anticipation of the epic set; since the history of the relationship which subsists in the principal group of characters is all focussed in the individual history of a single figure, Michael Henchard.

If I give an instance of the way in which the pattern of events weaves itself, in the novels of dramatic form, the reason for this classification will appear better than in any description. A very important turn is given to the plot of *The Return of the Native* by the mistake in the distribution of Mrs. Yeobright's guineas. Fifty guineas each should have gone to her niece Thomasin and her son Clym; by an accident, the whole hundred goes to Thomasin and nothing to Clym. This accident is most elaborately contrived. Mrs. Yeobright is unable or unwilling to visit either her niece or her son; and she entrusts the delivery of the two parcels to Christian Cantle, a man who occasionally works for her, and a faithful messenger

DRAMATIC FORM

enough, but rather light-headed. Cantle goes off with the parcels stowed in his boots, and meets some friends who are going to a bagman's raffle at the inn. There is no harm in his accompanying them; and, being assured that "there will be no uproar at all," and no " ba'dy gaieties," he goes to see the fun, and is easily persuaded to take part in the raffle, which is decided by dice. In a scene of admirable comedy, he wins the raffle; and, full of amazement and pride, and seeing no end to the fortune he may make, with a little practice, by this newly discovered talent of his, begs to be given the dice; which is allowed. Then he sets out in earnest on his errand; and this time he is accompanied by Wildeve, Thomasin's husband. Now Wildeve had previously offered to carry Mrs. Yeobright's gift to his wife, but had been refused; and he suspects that the half-wit Christian has been employed to do the thing for which he himself was not thought sufficiently trustworthy. Nettled at this, he maliciously stirs up his silly companion's new-found enthusiasm for gambling; and shortly the two are hard at it, dicing for Thomasin's guineas, at the pathside in the warm summer darkness, by the light of a candle. Wildeve wins Thomasin's fifty, and Cantle begins desperately to stake Clym's guineas; loses these too, and in crazy remorse rushes off into the night. Wildeve's intention had apparently been to distribute the guineas with his own hands as Mrs. Yeobright had intended; thus quietly rebuking her for not trusting him. But now appears on the scene the reddleman, Diggory Venn, Thomasin's faithful but disappointed lover. He has come up unobserved, has watched this queer midnight game of dice, and has taken the guineas, from half-heard snatches of Cantle's talk, to be all Thomasin's. Venn, like Mrs. Yeobright, thoroughly mistrusts Wildeve; and at once concludes to attempt winning back the money and himself carrying out Mrs. Yeobright's errand. He challenges Wildeve to continue the dicing, and, after much excitement, wins the whole hundred. Wildeve sullenly goes home; and Venn wraps the guineas up in a screw of paper and hands the whole lot of them to Thomasin; thus, with the best intention, turning Mrs. Yeobright's kindness to tragic misfortune, as it turns out.

Such construction as this may justly be called dramatic; its finely fitted joinery may well have been suggested by Hardy's loving study of Sophocles—evidently an influence scarcely second in importance to his architectural studies. This skilful and elaborate contriving of an accident in itself comparatively simple, power-

DRAMATIC FORM

fully excites and maintains the reader's interest. Briefly extracted from the book, the passage may appear to be the work of some artifice; it is possible to criticize the remarkable run of luck that falls first to Wildeve, then to Venn. But such things are known; any season at a casino might parallel it. And unquestionably in the story the most noticeable effect of this complicated pattern of events, is that the unfortunate accident falls out in a strangely inevitable way; so far from seeming artificial, the series of occurrences has a formidable air of unswerving destiny. Moreover, it enables the story to proceed in a succession, not simply of events, but of vivid and separate *scenes*, which the reader cannot resist imaginatively visualizing: the raffling in the public-house, the dicing by the pathside in lantern light and at last in glowworm light. What, however, is perhaps even more important for us to notice here, is that this accident, so contrived, becomes an occurrence not in the history of the one or two persons directly affected, but in the history of the relationship of a whole group of persons. The train of its happening, from Mrs. Yeobright to Clym, by including in its circuit the lives of Wildeve and Venn, and passing through them, involves the whole group in the business from the very beginning of it; binds the group firmer together, and adds something to the progressive fate of the whole relationship; and this is something more important to the form of the completed story than that which the misfortune adds to the individual fates of Clym and Mrs. Yeobright.

In three of these novels of dramatic form—*Far from the Madding Crowd, The Return of the Native, The Woodlanders*—there is an evident similarity of the human material used in them. The central group of characters in each is a set of four persons, two men and two women; and each group is composed of similar contrasts and similar resemblances. The tensions within the groups vary somewhat; and the characters, moulded by differing processes of external event, show differing developments. But the three stories begin with almost exactly the same set of ingredients; they are, in fact, three various experiments in the tragic compounding of the same ingredients. The similarity is especially noticeable in the case of the men. Gabriel Oak, Diggory Venn, and Giles Winterborne are clearly brothers; indeed, a family so identical in feature, physical, mental, and spiritual, is beyond the accomplishment of human generation. These three men are but three disguises of a single piece of psychological imagination; and the disguising is scarcely more

DRAMATIC FORM

than a difference in name, in trade, and fortune. But, though they are hardly more than three instances of one conception, it is a fine and dignified conception, which easily bears repetition. The steadfast lover, so faithful that personal disappointment is of no account matched with the welfare of the beloved, is the natural flowering here of "plain heroic magnitude of mind"; of a life whose whole conduct is simple unquestioning patience, a tolerant fortitude deeply rooted in the earth, and directly nourished by the imperceptible vigours of impersonal nature. Set off against Oak, Venn, and Winterborne, are three instances of one kind of contrast—Troy, Wildeve, and Fitzpiers: sharp intellects, genteel manners, inflammable faithless passions, shallow good-nature, and flashy disdain for rusticity. Except perhaps for Troy, these characters are not so firmly imagined as the figures they oppose; they have rather the air of being invented to provide the required opposition. But there is more variety in the detailed character of these genteel figures than in the contrasting set; though it is for the most part the variety shown by similar characters inhabiting different stations of life. They are, all three, unstable swaggering natures; but Troy, the bastard slip of a noble family, enlisted in the cavalry, has a romantic daring virility, trickster though he is, that finds no counterpart in the mean shiftiness of Wildeve, the engineer turned publican; and Fitzpiers, the unsuccessful doctor with a taste for metaphysics, is a creature of subtler passions than either of the others.

The female members of the three groups arrange themselves into similar oppositions: Bathsheba, Eustacia, and Grace Melbury, against Fanny Robin, Thomasin Yeobright, and Marty South; on the whole, capricious, passionate, self-conscious natures—not all impatient of their rural surroundings, but all interested chiefly in their own vanity and fineladyism—are set against patience, simplicity, and humility. But one has only to read through this list of names to be reminded that Hardy's psychological imagination is much better suited, in the main, to the creation of feminine than of masculine character. For as regards their heroines, these three novels have no similarity at all, except for each showing broadly the same kind of contrast. Each pair of opposites is far from repeating, in slightly varying terms, the same pair of psychological conceptions; Hardy's power of inventing feminine character has been able to effect a similar contrast in three completely different couples of antagonists, so that Bathsheba, Eustacia, and

DRAMATIC FORM

Grace repeat each other as little as Fanny, Thomasin, and Marty. Moreover, in the case of the men, Hardy has to show off the generous qualities of his faithful characters by making their opponents contemptible; but with the women, the complex personalities are as admirable as their simpler opposites, and often perhaps more lovable—unquestionably more commanding.

The chief human material, then, in each of these three novels, is a quartette of personalities, simple and complex, one of each quality in each sex. But the emotional tensions which bind these groups together are variously devised. The reader may be amused with some formulæ for these arrangements. Suppose we turn the personalities into algebra by putting A^1 for masculine simplicity, and A^2 for feminine simplicity, B^1 for masculine complexity and B^2 for feminine complexity; then (as the text-books say) we have:—

In *Far from the Madding Crowd*, A^1 loves B^2, who loves B^1, who loves A^2.

In *The Return of the Native*, A^1 loves A^2, who loves B^1, who loves B^2.

In *The Woodlanders*, A^2 loves A^1, who loves B^2, who loves B^1.

These formulæ stand for the groups as they

first definitely arrange themselves. The reader need not be too serious over this critical algebra; which is not without its use, however, in analysing the art of Hardy's fiction—an art made of too noble a stuff to be damaged by such mathematical abstraction. We see at once how each series of lovers, unable without dislocation to form a "closed chain," is deliberately arranged for tragedy. The system of emotional tensions does not, of course, remain the same through each novel; the tensions slacken, shift, or are broken off. Each book, in fact, narrates the history of a system of such tensions, almost as if this were an organism; and perhaps it is. The matter of the story is the response given to the processes of externality not simply by a group of individuals, but by the "sightless substance" of compounded emotion which the group creates, a substance which (a "*unanimiste*" would say) is itself an individual existence; it is something, at any rate, capable of receiving injury and invigoration from destiny.

But besides the varying arrangement within the groups, there is important modification of their system introduced by additional members in each of these three novels; and these have a function in each story as serious as that held by the representatives of the constant group. In *Far from the Madding Crowd*, the emotional

DRAMATIC FORM

system is complicated by the fiercely kindled Boldwood, in whose passionate heart love

> "flings about his burning heat
> As in a furnace an ambitious fire,
> Whose vent is stopt."

Mrs. Yeobright, with her formidable pride, and Clym, with his scepticism in worldly affairs and his sincere indifference to success, contribute notably to the tragic stuff of *The Return of the Native*. And Melbury, doubting whether to give his daughter, out of remorse, to Giles, or to give her to the taking and well-born Fitzpiers out of affectionate ambition, puts a pathetic bias on the emotional process of *The Woodlanders;* as, in the same book, Mrs. Charmond goes with Grace in the contrast of refined womanhood against Marty South's patience and rusticity, supplying the whole business with that element of capricious passion, the lack of which sets Grace clearly apart from Eustacia and Bathsheba. But we shall go very far wrong, if we suppose that any analysis of the emotional stresses, round which these novels are constructed, will give us the key to their whole result; we have, after all, only been examining their mechanics. It is, certainly, interesting and important to note, that in novels of such various complete result—rather, in novels which give such varying guise to the general significance underlying all Hardy's characteristic work—the art should be so similarly mechanized. But exactly what it is that this mechanism of complicated emotions works to produce, is not so easily seized into words. To be sure, we can say that the attitude to nature held by the persons in each central group, is as weighty in the whole effect as the composite plotting of emotions more easily describable—love, jealousy, enmity. For Gabriel Oak's or Marty South's willing immersion in the common life of earth, and Wildeve's or Eustacia's desire to be refined above it, easily stand symbolic of personality knowing itself carried down one endless universal tendency, now acquiescing in the current, now wilful against it. And this will sum up for us the general significance. Yet this takes us only a little way; for it is the *form* which the significance acquires that is the really important thing. Nothing less than the whole story, with all its complexity of character and emotion, its main trend and its minutely framed plot, its comedy and tragedy, its groundwork of vital earth—nothing less than all this will give us the real result; nothing less than the thing itself, in fact. Hardy's fiction, at its best, is like music in this; for what a piece of music really means

DRAMATIC FORM

is simply the music, and just so the whole meaning of the story is—the story. This is what the mastery of form, and nothing else, can do. Three books start with closely similar material, mechanized after exactly the same fashion, and yield, in the end, one characteristic significance. Yet the books are three essentially different works of art; for they are three expressions of formal mastery; and formal mastery never repeats itself.

In *Far from the Madding Crowd*, the story opens in the large air of pastoral life; the vivid description of a night of stars seen from a lonely hill-top, when the earth seems to be perceptibly swinging through the void, is an admirable prelude to the " sightless substance " of the tragedy, with its essential element of universal unalterable movement, just as the horrible disaster to Oak's flock preludes the material substance of the drama. But the story soon passes from this upland atmosphere, and remains in the placid, delicious region of farming life in the lowlands—Bathsheba Everdene's homestead, and the village of Weatherbury, set in the beautiful English fertility. The life is exciting enough in moments: witness the feverish trouble caused on that sleepy Sunday afternoon by the sheep breaking fence and invading a field of young clover—" and they be getting blasted . . . and will all die as dead as nits." But in the main it is a life quietly rich with sedate activity; this is the external condition which, combining with the emotional energies it surrounds and penetrates, like substance in a dissolving liquor, works out the unique complete result of the whole story. No book of Hardy's has such a wealth of profound and splendid comedy; the band of labourers—Joseph Poorgrass, Laban Tall, Mark Clark, Matthew Moon, Henery Fray, Jan Coggan, the old malter and young Cain Ball—is an achievement which, for easy inspiration of genius, can only be matched in the very greatest literature. In several scenes the elemental comedy of these rustic immortals is without doubt Shakespearean in degree as well as in kind; in the scene, for instance, when Joseph Poorgrass and Jan Coggan are drinking together while the body of poor Fanny Robin lies on the waggon outside. And this comedy is woven into the tragedy with exquisite discretion. The tragedy (it must be called so, in spite of its peaceful close) is, of course, dominated by the spirited, wilful figure of Bathsheba—Bathsheba, whose caprice is responsible for the death of Troy and the worse than death of Boldwood, who, though not overtly rebellious against her surroundings, is implicitly so by her ladyish delicacy, and yet is, we must surely admit, thoroughly worthy of Oak's dogged and tireless adoration: a figure in which feminine charm and feminine destructiveness are wonderfully mingled.

Eustacia, in *The Return of the Native*, is a more impressive, but much less charming figure. She does not, indeed, charm at all—it is not in her nature; she conquers and commands. Wilfulness becomes stormy passion in her, caprice turns to scornful determination to have in all things no law but her own nature. And yet there is a gloomy readiness in her to take the smallest adverse turn in her fortune as evidence of an immense malicious fate arrayed against her. The process of things is not for her a blind chance-medley of onward motions; the world is a huge deliberate conspiracy, consciously inventing devices for her ruin: nothing less than this will her pride believe in; for her nature is tragic, and she must be the centre of her universe. Hence this tragic fiction of her own insatiable pride for ever threatens her; and she for ever looks it down with fierce contempt. There is grandeur in this perverse, unhappy woman. If Sue Bridehead is the subtlest of Hardy's feminine characters, Eustacia Vye has the deepest force. She is one of those figures who are not only themselves, but their own incarnate destiny. They are in a world which is a tragic poetry of their own creation; for it is a world made by "submitting the shows of things to the desires of the mind," and these are the dangerous desires for self-importance, which find a heady satisfaction in standing upright and unconquerable against a world of enmity. And so the tragic poetry of their own notional world at last overwhelms them; since they are unconsciously bent towards those actions whose result is likely to make their actual world conform to the world of their imaginative pride. Such is Eustacia. And the story she moves in has an atmosphere altogether suited to her. There is admirable comedy in it; but not quite of such quality as that of *Far from the Madding Crowd*, not comedy that searches life as deeply as tragedy itself. Neither is it so broadly distributed, being chiefly provided by Christian Cantle with his starts and terrors, and old Grandfer Cantle, absurdly industrious in jocularity, and as absurdly vainglorious, especially on the militarism of his youth: "there wasn't a finer figure in the whole South Wessex than I, as I looked when dashing past the shop-windows with the rest of our company on the day we ran out o' Budmouth because it was thoughted that Boney had landed round the point." These lighter passages

DRAMATIC FORM

scarcely interrupt the steady process of the tragedy, and certainly nothing dilute its constant intensity. Egdon Heath, with all its sights and sounds so vividly and inescapably imagined, presides over the story, a vast, careless oppression. In no book of Hardy's is the ceaseless drifting power of material fate so impressively or so directly typified — neither malignant nor benevolent, but simply indifferent, unconscious of its freightage of a humanity not so much struggling as vainly desiring against its relentless motion. And Eustacia, by so pitiably mistaking the indifference of its motion for malignity, does actually turn it into malignity on herself and on the others: tragedy the inevitable answer to personality's self-assertion against the impersonal power of the world—the fundamental tragedy of the human state, according to this metaphysic. The book goes through an astonishing series of memorable scenes: the bonfire; Eustacia on the heath alone, or disguised among the mummers; the dicing by the roadside; Mrs. Yeobright's death from the adder's sting; Susan's magic image. The story is one that cannot be merely read; to the feeblest imagination, it must surely act itself in clearest visualization.

In *The Woodlanders* the story is placed under

the dominance of a much more kindly aspect of nature; but the dominance is scarcely less masterful. The villagers are drencht by the subtle influence of their surrounding woods. Melbury's infatuated fears for the gentility of his well-educated daughter finely realize this; he is anxious not only of the effect rustic manners, and seclusion from the nice world, may have on her—"her bounding walk becoming the regular Hintock shail-and-wamble"—but of the formidable assimilating power of the earth, of which he himself is perfectly conscious: "we, living here alone, don't notice how the whitey-brown creeps out of the earth over us," as he quaintly puts it; but he knows quite well that the "whitey-brown" *does* creep over him, and not only over clothes and skin, but into mind and spirit. The book, however, is full of a profound penetration of humanity by nature; Marty South's father, whose life was strangely linked to the life of a tree, which he feared, but could not survive, is the obvious type of it. But Marty South herself, and Giles Winterborne, both suffering bitter frustration of personal desire, but both deeply acquiescing in the process of impersonal life that has them in its power—these two are the characters who, more than any others, give the book its special quality. And these two, who have the chief

DRAMATIC FORM

share of the elements of Hardy's tragedy—unyielding personal desire, mixt with the sense of frustrating impersonal life carrying them forward—are the characters whom events most severely punish; Giles for loving the refined Grace, Marty for loving Giles, and both for being steadfast in love. From often working together among the trees, the two have a vast common knowledge of nature's ways in woodland earth; but Marty's is the more delicate apprehension; it is she, for instance, who notices that the young pines begin to sigh as soon as they are held upright: "they sigh because they are very sorry to begin life in earnest." Marty, indeed, is by far the greatest and noblest of Hardy's types of simple-natured womanhood. Her psychology is an imagination as inspired as that of Eustacia herself; and for sheer beauty of character there is no one like her through all the Wessex Novels. Sorrow and bitter hard work and humiliation have been with her all her life; but the sweetness of her mind and the iron endurance of her spirit are not to be hurt by such things. Her sense of coming tragedy is utterly different from Eustacia's; she quietly knows that pain will reward such love as hers; but she will neither try to escape it nor go to meet it; whatever happens, her unalterable love is her own. The tragedy of the book is subdued compared with that of *The Return of the Native;* but it has a terribly moving climax in the death of Giles, and a close of keenest pathos, of sorrow intolerably sweet, in Marty's lament over his grave. He must have eyes of horn who can read the words of her exalted, yet exquisitely poignant grief, with no mist troubling his sight. I think we should have to go to Wordsworth, to find a great, settled depth of emotion expressed with more perfect simplicity, than in this last speech of Marty's, ending with a praise of goodness that all unconsciously praises her own most beautiful quality: "If ever I forget your name let me forget home and heaven! . . . But no, no, my love, I never can forget 'ee; for you was a good man, and did good things!"—It is a good woman who speaks so.

In none of these three novels is there a consistently central character; the central subject, as I have said, is rather the emotional relationship combining a group of persons, and the changes caused in this relationship by a current of events; though there are degrees of personal force in the members of each group. But in *The Life and Death of the Mayor of Casterbridge,* the last but one, in order of publication, of the novels I have called dramatic, there is a distinct change in the manner of the conception.

DRAMATIC FORM

The title hints at the change; and still more the sub-title; for this is the "story of a man of character." Here, then, it is the strength of a single person that is to be submitted to a process of impersonal event; it is the tragedy of one man, not of a group. His is the life through which the ceaseless electricity of universal force is to be shown pouring; much more evidently through him, at least, than through a circuit of several lives. And it is his spirit that is to resist with its own desires the fatal energy of general existence, burning to incandescence with its resistance, and at last broken with its burning. To this concentration on the life of a single individual, Hardy's fiction was, it seems, naturally tending; though *The Woodlanders* comes after it, *The Mayor of Casterbridge* shows the change from dramatic fiction to the epic fiction of *Tess of the D'Urbervilles* and *Jude the Obscure* to be, not a sudden jump, but a gradual development. For in *The Mayor of Casterbridge*, Hardy is still held by his dramatic style of construction. In its conception, the story really concerns Michael Henchard alone; but the book is engined with the familiar group-mechanism of the three other novels. The construction obeys the necessity of keeping the group fastened together and all concerned in the history; but it is Henchard's history, and for that the whole construction, and the other members of the group, properly exist. This is not at all like what occurs in the other dramatic novels. The group, however, is still substantially the same; at any rate, it is made up of similar kinds of opposition, though these cannot fall into a similar series of emotional stresses, since one member of the group of four principals is the daughter of another. But Lucetta is evidently on Eustacia's side, as Elizabeth Jane is on Thomasin's; and the rough vigour of Henchard is contrasted with, and opposed to, Farfrae's cleverness and nicety, very much as Diggory Venn is against Wildeve. In the psychology of the two male characters in this group, however, there is no repetition of the other groups. Farfrae is an excellent good fellow, and worthily engages the affections of those who know him; Gabriel Oak could not be further from shifty dealing or flighty passion. For any injury Henchard takes from him, the fault certainly does not lie with Farfrae. And Henchard is only to be compared with the simple-natured men in the other three groups, for the unconscious primitive strength which he seems to draw, like them, straight from the earth. Oak, Venn, and Winterborne are static characters; but Henchard is above everything dynamic, and there are forces in him of much

DRAMATIC FORM

greater depth and much greater variety than in any of the others.—To the central group of four chief figures, other figures are more or less loosely attached: Susan Henchard, pathetic nonentity; Newson, the genial trusting sailor; and the furmity-seller, the haggish destiny in Henchard's tragedy.

The processes of nature, which are so carefully and vividly, and with such obvious symbolic purport, mingled into the substance of the three other dramatic novels, are scarcely present in *The Mayor of Casterbridge*. But they are not needed; Henchard himself takes their place. He is, probably, the greatest instance of masculine characterization in Hardy's fiction; Jude's history may be the more significant, but Jude is conceived in a narrower mould than Henchard. He himself altogether provides the two main elements which combine to produce tragedy. In the rest of Hardy's fiction, these tragic elements are, on the whole, separately provided, by personality, and by the circumstances which have hold of personality. But the elemental antinomy, which is the basis of Hardy's tragedy, is entirely Henchard's own; the antinomy of the ruthless driving forward of the main unappointed force of being, against the vitality which has become formulated into an organism of conscious desire. Henchard's conscious aspirations are undone by the impetuous stream of unconscious vigour which his own being provides, and fatally provides. So he himself appears as the symbolic counterpart of the whole tragic substance of the other dramatic novels. There, that substance is chiefly compounded of inner and outer forces; though certainly the outer impersonal force has always a strong alliance in that impersonal region which surrounds the consciousness of every human creature, and yet is included in individual existence. But in Henchard, human nature's dualism of personal and impersonal force is so intensified that his whole circumstance, as far as it is injurious to him, seems but the objectification of his own self-injuring nature. The significance of *The Mayor of Casterbridge* is, therefore, in every way a notable variation on the general theme of Hardy's dramatic fiction.

Henchard, however, besides the deep primal discord of his nature, has, within the boundaries of his consciousness, a great deal of complexity; or perhaps it were better said, of variety; for it is a character above everything straightforward. But the surprising turns his conduct takes all have the effect, once they have happened, not of confusing but of confirming the definition of his personality. His first passionate affection for Farfrae changes into a sulky admission that

DRAMATIC FORM

clever wits will go farther than untaught vigour; and this in turn causes him suddenly to force Farfrae into rivalship, desperately determined to prove himself the better man; and having made a rival of Farfrae, he furiously hates him for the treachery to their early friendship, which is entirely his own doing: it is all inevitable. Then there is a sort of fierce honour in the man. His hatred of Farfrae would go to any length; but when he deliberately attempts to kill him, it must be by fair fight, and he pinions his own arm to lessen the advantage of his strength. This is an astonishing stroke of character-drawing; and it is finely supported by other incidents; when, for instance, Lucetta pitiably puts herself in his power, and to ruin her would be also to ruin the detested Farfrae, Henchard scornfully throws her letter on the fire. Indeed, when we are examining this book, the superb psychology of Michael Henchard yields such a fascination, that we are tempted to think his character the essence of the story. But it is no more this, than is the striking series of scenes and incidents through which the story moves: Henchard's selling his wife in the furmity-tent—surely one of the most cogent beginnings of narrative in the world—; the skimmity-ride; Susan Henchard's death, with the pennies she provided to weigh down her eyelids (pennies which Christopher Coney dug up and drank), and her direction to "open the windows as soon as I am carried out," and that fine elegy from wicked old Mother Cuxsom (" and all her shining keys will be took from her, and her cupboards opened; and little things 'a didn't wish seen, anybody will see "); the boosy conversations of Mixen Lane; and so on. Art like Thomas Hardy's fiction is not to be abstracted in analyses of plot and character. The story, with all its detail, and the inevitable process of Henchard's history, from the sin that braces him with remorse to make some good of life, through the heights of his prosperity, down to the anguished resignation confessed in his scribbled will—the story is a great particular instance, put into objective formality, of the tragic metaphysic behind a noble artist's conception of the world. It is not one man's old sin finding him out; but a type of the general sin of personal existence, and personal desire, in a universe of indifferent fate. And the tragedy is not so much punishment exacted for this, as the stubborn endurance of the punishment. But just how this formal typification is done, is only to be seen in the whole story itself.

VI

EPIC FORM

TESS OF THE D'URBERVILLES: JUDE THE OBSCURE

In dramatic art, whether cast as a novel or as a play, the materials, besides forming a vivid picture of familiar existence, may easily be moulded into some close conspiracy to express the author's peculiar way of understanding the world and the human state in it. But in any kind of drama—concerned as it must be with a definite and intricate complex of personalities, and needing all its formal power to hold the history of that turbulent and struggling stuff within some shapeliness of enclosure—it is in the highest degree inconvenient, scarcely to be managed without notable injury to the form, to make overt declaration of the sense in which the author takes his own apprehension of the world; whether, namely, life, in this conception of his, seems to him a bad business or something cordially acceptable. Human nature may be *dramatized* in an exact and (in the art) altogether credible co-ordination with some conceived relationship of the finite being of persons to the infinite being of the universe; and yet the result may—and indeed almost certainly must—leave room for further conclusions; for what our emotions, our sense of justice and of ultimate fitness, are to make of it all: how, in fact, we are to *feel* the whole result. Granted that we may receive, say, Macbeth, or the Duchess of Malfy, or Brand, or Michael Henchard, as artistically true presentation of life, the dramatic art nevertheless leaves it an open question, whether life so represented is to be desired or n't; the question must be answered personally, as if it were put by life itself. But there are artists who are unable to remain content with an art which holds this strictly judicial attitude to their own conclusions; their summing up of life's conduct strongly moves them, one way or another; and this also at last demands artistic expression.

Herein, it appears, lies the secret of Hardy's change from fiction of dramatic to fiction of epic form. The æsthetic manner of those four great novels, which the last chapter considered, admirably enabled him to express his intellectual conception of life, from its outer show of events to the inmost primal discord of its nature, and even to the necessary tragic resolution of the discord. But it withheld him from adding to

EPIC FORM

his formation of life the gloss of his own opinion of the tragedy. That tragedy is not an accidental accompaniment of life, but essential to its nature, this manner of art can be brought, without any violence, to assert; but it is very difficult for it to assert either that the tragedy is a fine, heartening business or, on the contrary, pitiable and unjust. Already, in *The Mayor of Casterbridge*, Hardy appears somewhat restive under the restriction; the book seems several times on the verge of indignantly protesting against the injustice of Henchard's fate—a fate which gave his personality a wealth of striving, aspiring vigour, and then punished him for possessing the gift. One has the feeling that the art is here constantly hoping to be able to do something which the artist's conscience will not tolerate. So a change of æsthetic habit becomes necessary, and *Tess of the D'Urbervilles* and *Jude the Obscure* are written in a form which the artist's conscience easily allows to contain an emotional as well as an intellectual judgment of life.

The term "epic," for the form in which these two novels are cast, is only meant as a convenient label; I shall not attempt meticulously to make good its propriety. Still, something must be said to indicate how this form, whatever we call it, enables fiction to go further than presenting objective life in co-ordination with an intellectual conception of its inmost manner of existence; to add, in fact, the result, in the author's own emotions, of this conception. Instead of being constructed round a progressive harmony of several individual themes, the form of these two novels develops a single theme, the life-history of one person, and sends this uninterruptedly forward. This is obviously the case in *Tess of the D'Urbervilles;* not quite so obviously in *Jude the Obscure*, for Sue Bridehead is a character drawn with as exact and penetrating a care as Jude himself. Yet she is only the subject of the book in so far as she affects Jude; with him the story begins and ends, and the whole form of the book is moulded to his single history. In both the dramatic and the epic kinds of novel, the separate events in which the personal theme is clothed yield a common unity of general event, by all obeying one presiding interest; so that in both forms the events make a continuous and shapely series, cemented together by mutual influence. But it is in the series of the events that the mere difference of intricacy between the two forms becomes so important to artistic capacity. In order to keep a closely related complex, made of several human lives, moving uniformly through a story, the events which

EPIC FORM

carry it cannot merely march forward, one evolving from another in a straight line of progress; they must not only act forwards, but to each side as well, and simultaneously. It is not a string, but rather a riband of events, that is required; there must be a firm continuity from end to end, and also, and quite as importantly, there must be firm weaving at every stage *across* the line of events, a close texture of breadth as well as of length. Scarcely anything of this, however, is required for an epic kind of novel. With only the history of a single life to carry, there needs but continuity of events from end to end; the complex cross-weaving of events, transversely to the main onward line of progress, is not wanted. In the dramatic novels, therefore, with their intricate linkages of events both lengthways and crossways, formal control finds a pretty full employment in keeping the mere matter of the story in order, and has about as much as it can do to relate the matter intellectually with the artistic metaphysic of the whole, leaving the emotional relation for inference. But in the matter of the epic novels, formal control is freed from a good deal of this employment, and can without much risk take definitely within its scope that which dramatic form must let go; with a less intricate texture of substance, more of the intangible stuff can be woven in, and closely complicated with it. The *breadth* of event, which takes up so much room in dramatic form, leaves room in epic form for a greater accompanying breadth of significance. For we may image the *material* progress of the story by likening it to a procession of ships down a strait; if the ships go forward in a broad front, formed at right angles to the direction of their sailing, the whole movement of the procession will have covered most of the space of the water. But if the ships go in a single or a narrow line, there will be a space on either side of their path which their movement has not occupied. Perhaps this diagram seems to make containing form too much a thing of fixt artifice; but it is quite fair to represent the difference between the two forms as a question of *room*—room left by the procession of material events, which may therefore be filled by the "sightless substance." Alternatively, however, we might say, that the dramatic form is like a string quartette, the epic form like a solo violin: it is in the solo that we most easily hear the quality of tone caused by *overtones*. So, in the epic novels, a great tune is played on a single human life; and because there is only one instrument, we are able to hear, instead of the harmony of human living, the whole quality of the one instrument's tone, all its intellectual and emotional overtones.

It is clear, at any rate, that, when we pass from the four novels discussed in the last chapter, to the two which we here consider, we must soon understand the change to a simpler, more direct form to be the sign of a change in the whole condition of the art,—of a change to a more intricate intention with regard to significance. The objective life in these two novels is shown as a phenomenon much more closely and intensely "complicated with the life beyond"—with the life of its author, namely—than in the others. Humanity is still the same restless affair of personal desires asserting themselves against the vast unconcerned current of existence; the tragedy is still man's refusal to be held in the process of mere general being, and his inability to make his refusal prevail. But the inevitable agony is not only set forth in these two books; it is judged. If man has his intellect, which enables him so to conceive the manner of his existence, he also has his sense of justice; and it enables him, rather compels him, to see this existence of his as a harsh and senseless violation of his profoundest belief—the belief that his sense of justice *ought* to be satisfied. Such, in brief, is the burden of these two books' significance. It is, of course, not a new significance, but only the complete working out, as far as it can be carried, of the prime antagonism between the desires of personality and the forces of its existence—worked out simultaneously in artistic statement of life, and of the author's attitude to his own statement. In fact, it is a modern version of the oldest and most unshakable of all religious or philosophical doctrines, the doctrine of original sin, of the fatal antinomy between man's nature and the divine impulse of the world: for perception of this is the origin of the doctrine. Only, in this modern version, the tragic punishment of the antinomy is not made out to be man's due for wilful transgression of the divine world's nature. It is certainly man's self-will that causes the antinomy; but did man make himself self-willed?—By some kink or eddy in the pouring forces of the world, existence has produced within it the self-willed vortex of man's personality; the exercise of self-will is the prime necessity of his being, for without that he is no more man; but, through being utterly immersed in the huge onward speed of general existence, his self-will, that seems always to promise the achievement of some movement of *his own*, is for ever contradicted. So the only final result of self-will for man, is that the unrelenting motion of fate becomes a tyrannous agony; his continued existence is a tragedy without purpose and without end—" the

EPIC FORM

end? there is no end: the end is death and madness." Hence, throughout these two books, the atmosphere is charged with a fierce indignation against the fundamental injustice of man's existence. Tess is described, in the title of her history, with challenging defiance, as "a pure woman faithfully presented"; but the protest for which this prepares us, is not uttered against the stupid logic of society. That, to be sure, is pilloried; but much more than that; Tess's tragedy is a specimen syllogism in the cruel reasoning of universal fate. Her tortured life, unnecessarily sensitive, is nothing but the symbolic language wherein the premisses of fate are quietly and ruthlessly worked out; and it is the useless fact that she *is* sensitive—that fate, for its rapt arguing with itself, has invented the medium of human life, utterly careless that it is a medium exquisitely tormented by the processes of this transcendent reasoning—it is this useless fact which stirs Hardy to fill the record of her life, not with pathos or pity, but with irreconcilable indignation against the prime, tragic condition of life. It is the same with Jude: his history of baffled aspiration is like an argument fate holds with itself, intensely reasoning whether man's personal effort can have any final value in the course of its own existence, calling Jude's sensitive life into being merely to put the endless problem in another instance, deciding the case with regard only to its own logic, and for its own dialectic satisfaction, caring in no way for the resulting passage of agony through Jude's conscious nerves. Indeed, we can hardly read these two disturbing books without feeling that their accusing passion is in them not merely on behalf of the lives they imagine; they surely confess, under the covert fiction of their histories, their author's personal sense of life, of its tragic compound of individual desire and the overriding force of general existence: "hinc indignatur se mortalem esse creatum."

Both these novels, on their first appearance, roused a certain amount of public opposition, and even resentment. It is, perhaps, hardly worth while to remember this; but it seems likely that the cause of it was not so much the matter of the two tragedies (though this was ostensibly attacked), as their passionate spirit of indignation with the deep condition of life, their fierce arraignment of the world which life must inhabit. The mood called pessimism is common enough in modern poetry; but there it is not very troublesome to the general reading public. Pessimism in novels, however, is a different matter; and when a great and popular novelist like Thomas Hardy seemed to devote all the resources of his art to presenting a thoroughly pessimistic view of the world, the reading public was perturbed, and protested, as though there had been some breach of faith. This attitude can scarcely be dismissed by superior sneering. There is sound instinct in it; but the instinct is adulterated with stupidity,—the stupidity of a nation which, at one period the most naturally artistic in Europe, has so debased itself with industry that it has lost most of its imagination, and therewith the faculty of self-projection, without which art may be admired, but scarcely at all appreciated. Still, objection to the spirit in which *Tess of the D'Urbervilles* and *Jude the Obscure* are written, deserves to be in some sort answered. The objection is based on the common belief—which, simple as it is, cannot easily be controverted—that art must have, in one way or another, a utilitarian value: it ought to be of some good to us. So it ought; but the good that art can do is not to be judged by the good that other things can do. If we do not let a work of art entirely absorb us, and judge of everything in it by its relation to the whole; if we take so-and-so out of its artistic context, and consider how it would frame if fitted into our common wont of living: then we are certainly not judging art; we are even, through failure of self-projection, preventing art from doing us the good it might do. Allowing for a moment that the prevailing mood of these two novels is pessimistic; and allowing further that pessimism is a thing injurious to our common wont of life; even so, it by no means follows that the art which contains this mood may not be wonderfully good for us. The materials which an art employs are not the art itself. There are those who object to stories and plays, if their characters are bad lots; but it is just as irrelevant to object to them for containing some emotional significance we do not care about. We must first completely enter into the art; indeed, we must *become* the art; and then see whether we care about what the questionable stuff does in the art. If a work of art so uses its materials, whatever they be, as to give us some great and severe experience for imagination; then we have no right to ask anything more of it.

The truth is, that great art cannot ever be itself pessimistic, however much pessimism may go to its making. For the art itself is not to be produced without a vital exultation in him who produces it. It is not only "the shows of things submitted to the desires of the mind," but conquered, transfigured, completely sublimated by the desires of the mind. And the artist's exulting sense of life, the mastery of his formative imagination over the shows of things, and even over the significance he draws from them—this is the first and fundamental thing we feel in any real appreciation of art. Leopardi has poems which terribly question the virtue of being alive; but even while they are doing so, life's achievement, in such noble art, of a superb mastery over things, is rousing conscious life to triumph in us. The pessimists themselves, when they are honest with themselves, admit this paradox. "The City of Dreadful Night" is the declaration of one to whom life was profoundly evil. But why should the declaration be made at all? Thomson himself gives the reason:

> "Because it gives some sense of power and passion
> In helpless impotence to try to fashion
> Our woe in living words howe'er uncouth."

"Some sense of power and passion in helpless impotence"; yes, but the sense is the thing here. In the art, the sense of power and passion *is* power and passion. Even over woe and helpless impotence, formative imagination, the central vigour of man's nature, has won to mastery; it has fashioned it in strong and shapely art. And for him who receives the art, no less than for him who makes it, the deepest and most unquestionable result in work of large and prevailing formality, is the sense of command and power in life; a thing sufficiently removed from pessimism, however pessimistic the materials used may seem. Man's profound desire for order, system, linked significance, in his rough experience of the world, is completely satisfied in the firm shaping of art; immersed in it, he feels his will penetrating the world; and conscious mastery is added to his nature. And it often happens, that the more the art is removed from comfortable things, the more invigorated and severely delighted will the sense of mastery be: even a dread of existence, man can command, and put forth mastered into form. So it is with these two great novels of Thomas Hardy's. We may call their mood pessimistic, but they themselves are nothing so; for their art is altogether too shapely, too assured, too masterful. Yet the mood sometimes escapes from the art; in several passages it cries out uncontrolled; the final paragraph in *Tess of the D'Urbervilles* is a notable instance. And whether the mood be a thing we like or not, these passages are offensive; but simply because the form has given way, the art for a moment has lost its mastery.

Is it so certain, however, that even the mood of these two novels is pessimistic? I cannot understand it to be really so. A genuine pessimism must surely go further than the conception of existence as an evil; it must add to this

EPIC FORM

a sad acquiescence in the evil,—since what good can come of anything else than acquiescence, if all things end in evil? But the mood which governs *Tess of the D'Urbervilles* and *Jude the Obscure* is plainly not an acquiescence. It is a fierce, burning revolt against the evil it conceives. To accuse, and passionately to accuse, the measureless injustice of man's state in the world, is certainly to confess tacitly that it is worth while having a sense of justice; nay, that it is good to exercise one's sense of justice. And without doubt it is good—good for life, and for the consciousness of life. For even while existence is being arraigned as an unjust evil, the sense of justice is thereby impassioned to a flame of activity, profoundly *enjoying* itself and its own warmth, and sending the glow of its indignation through the whole consciousness that contains it. And so long as this is possible, so long as a conception of the world can do good to the sense of life, though it be only in this somewhat perverted fashion, I do not see that there can be genuine pessimism. But it must be admitted, and it already has been admitted,[1] that in these later novels of Hardy's there are some moments of unmistakable pessimism, when even the sense of justice coldly and dully confesses that it is not worth while to be outraged

[1] See page 29.

by the world it contemplates. Fortunately, these moments are few. But after all, the main thing is, that this mood of indignation against the tragic manner of human existence should be perfectly wrought into the *form* of the art; should not be allowed naked or unmanaged outcry, but should be conveyed by the whole nature of the art in which it is expressed. And on the whole, this is what happens.

" Poor wounded name ! " quotes the title-page of *Tess of the D'Urbervilles*, " my bosom as a bed shall lodge thee." Indeed, there are few books written with such intensity of personal feeling. The book has been accused of defending a thesis; but criticism could not be more inept. Neither does it defend Tess; for what is there in that lovely nature that needs defence? To defend the characters whom he creates is not a dignified attitude for a novelist to assume; and Hardy's fiction is always dignified. The person in this story who stands most in need of defence, is Angel Clare; and, fortunately for the art of the book, he does not get it. But what the story does for Tess, is to accept her with all the perfect sympathy and understanding of love. A charity that is infinitely larger than forgiveness accompanies her, loving her weakness as well as her strength, exquisitely understanding how her beautiful nature is forced by agony

EPIC FORM

into crime. It is decidedly uncommon in a work of art, such intense and personal regard on the part of the author for his own creation; and it is likely that this is what upset, and perhaps still upsets, the critical balance of some readers. But this noticeable dualism in *Tess of the D'Urbervilles* is exceedingly important for the conveying of the epic motive of the whole book—the dualism of a merciless, unhesitating tragic imagination, and an impotent fervour of charity for its central figure; charity that seems always desiring to protect this figure from the steady, injurious process of the imagination which conceived her, yet can do nothing but painfully watch her destruction. For so the whole content of the book's form, from the first materials of its story to the limits of their surrounding emotional significance, is pervaded by the conflict of two forces—" the inherent will to enjoy, and the circumstantial will against enjoyment." This conflict throughout the story, and through all its intellectual and emotional accompaniments, is graspt by a great epic unity of form. It is worked out in the simplest and barest manner, but in a spacious design, and with terrible earnestness. The story is not one of any complex human action; it does not deal with any daring aspiration, hardly with any notable motive. Tess's "will to enjoy" is nothing extravagant; there is no hardihood in it, which the relentless assimilating forces of worldly destiny might seize on and punish for its boldness. She merely hopes, modestly and humbly, for the happiness in life which her instincts seem to promise her; and it is for those instincts, implanted in her, that she is destroyed by anguish and crime. Thus the tragic idea of the world, which underlies all Hardy's work, finds in this book its simplest, and therefore its most terrible statement. Without any exciting turns or ingenious devices of narrative, Tess's history goes greatly and quietly forward, with a motion that mesmerizes by its deliberate unceasing pace; and it is the history of personality compelled, by its very nature, to utter its own desires against the immense unperturbed current of general existence, that takes no alteration from the personalities it sweeps forward. Scarcely anything in the story competes for the reader's interest with the austere driving-forward of the main epic theme. The characterization is just sufficiently elaborated to be real and substantial, and to give the theme definiteness and human particularity. There are no curious subtleties, nor searching into the secrets, of psychology. Tess herself would not make such a draft upon our affections, were it not for her tragic destiny: it is not so much for her character, as for the

EPIC FORM

fact that such a character should be so cruelly entreated, that we love her; though certainly there are few women in fiction, or for that matter in drama, of such beautifully lucid nature. Her parents are both admirably drawn; the sottish father, unable, without help from alcohol, to bear the weight of his family's antique greatness, and the genial, stupid, feckless mother, are as real as may be, and the story takes some splendid comedy from them, though the humour of it comes in rather sadly. But they are only characterized just as much as the great theme requires; they are strictly a part of its formal apparatus, and, you might say, know their place in the story, never intruding too much on the reader's attention. So also is it with the group of Tess's girl-companions at Talbothays; exquisitely real figures, these, but if one examines one's knowledge of them, it is plain that their natures are only just known enough to be distinct personalities. The only psychological surprise in the book is Alec D'Urberville's conversion from a lecher to a ranter. It is a fine stroke, but not a subtle one; a piece of broad rather than of searching psychology. His is not a nature capable of any profound development, and he would be less suited to the story if he were. His first sight of Tess after he has begun his preaching shows that he has but found a razor-edge footing on the heights of religion. After his question: "But since you wear a veil to hide your good looks, why don't you keep it down?"—we know well enough that his feet are slipping already; he will soon fall down, plump into the mire where he belongs. Yet he is as near to agony as such gross stuff can come, and has almost the touch of tragedy on him, when he cries out, "There never were such eyes, surely, before Christianity or since." Withal, he is a common enough sort of creature; but a common thing wrought with masterly art.

Angel Clare is the one figure in the book who is at all out of the ordinary run of human nature. His squeamish, fastidious nature, conscious of his own purity and unconscious of his deep insincerity, mixing with farm-hands as an equal and always feeling his own superiority, pretentiously broad-minded and essentially mean, is analysed with considerable care. He is not so pushed forward as to be too noticeable, however; though he is undoubtedly real enough to be odious. In fact, he is the only one of Hardy's characters who is genuinely odious. Even if one knew all about Alec D'Urberville, one could bear to have dinner with him; yes, and even those starched ninnyhammers, Angel's two parsonical brothers, might be agreeably

EPIC FORM

talked to at a garden-party. But no decent person, knowing Angel's history, would house with him or, if possible, talk with him. For he is theoretical high-mindedness; and than this there is nothing more disgusting, let alone its cruelty when it gets any actual life into its power. He, and not her seducer, is the real poison in Tess's life. Whether, when the story ends, he is to marry 'Liza-Lu, is not quite clear; Hardy seems to have shrunk from definitely adding to the sorrow of the book's close a piece of tragic irony similar to the comic irony with which the "Alchemist" ends. But I am sure he does marry her, and generously trains her to his standards; I am sure, at any rate, that the rest of his life is not much tormented with the pangs of self-contempt. Yet Angel Clare is profoundly necessary to the whole art of the book. If, for the sake of a moment's convenience, we allow ourselves roughly to allegorize the story, then Tess will be the inmost purity of human life, the longing for purity which has its intensest instinct in virginity; and Alec D'Urberville is "the measureless grossness and the slag" which inevitably takes hold of life, however virginal its desires. This is bad enough; it is a type of the fundamental tragedy of life. But the tragedy could be endured. It is Angel Clare who turns it to unendurable agony; for he is the venom not so much of self-consciousness as of introspection, horribly exaggerating the tragedy, adding that dreadful element, the idea of remorse, taking enforced impurity as a personal sin, cruelly *blaming* life for that the helpless fact of its existence does not equal its desires. And introspection is a no less essential part of the whole human tragedy, as this book has to declare it, than anything else therein.

But we must only play with this sort of allegorizing fantasy when we are considering a book of such human reality as this. We can extract, perhaps, a good deal of its significance, and analyse its narrative substance; but it is the epic unity of the book that is its greatest and noblest quality. No more than the intellectual and human elements in it, do the successive incidents blur with too much forwardness the severe gradual shaping of the whole; not even when they are so poignant as Tess's christening of her baby, or so charming as Clare carrying the dairymaids across the flooded stream. The scenery of the story is equally obedient to its whole emotional process. The descriptions are done with extraordinarily minute intensity; but their innumerable detail is fused by a continuous and large design, so that a multitude of small strokes builds up a spacious background of living earth for the human events. Except for *The Return of the Native,* no other novel of Hardy's has its action *placed* so grandly, and with such perfect propriety. And whereas the dramatic stories have in the main a fixt and unaltering background, here, as seems proper to the epic movement, the setting alters with the progressive emotion of the story, turning bleaker and harsher as the tragic stress deepens. It is with a more than logical propriety, that the scenery of Tess's life changes from the prodigal beauty of the Vales of Blackmoor and Froom, to the grim upland winter of Flintcomb Ash, with its hard soil immensely exposed to scathing rain and windy snow; and that her occupation correspondingly changes from idyllic dairying under the humorous Crick (with his delightful stories of William Dewey fiddling to the bull and Jack Dollop hiding in the churn), to aching toil among the swedes, at reed-drawing, and on the threshing machine, under the eye of a vindictive curmudgeon. And perhaps it is not unduly forcing the epithet to claim an epic quality for much of the dialogue—for its simplicity and directness, for the way it conveys the circumstance of the story in the habit of its imagery, and especially for the way the brooding motive of the whole business speaks through the various characters; in, for instance, such a speech as this:

THOMAS HARDY

" Her mind can no more be heaved from that one place where it do bide than a stooded waggon from the hole he's in. Lord love 'ee, neither court-paying, nor preaching, nor the seven thunders themselves, can wean a woman when 'twould be better for her that she should be weaned."

From first to last, *Tess of the D'Urbervilles* is one relentless onward movement. The human narrative, the surrounding nature, the accompaniment of intellectual and emotional significance, all weave inextricably together, and go forward dominated by a unity of purpose; they unite in a single epic statement, formidable in its bare simplicity, of the conflict between personal and impersonal—the conflict which is the inmost vitality of all Hardy's noblest work.

If we may regard *Tess of the D'Urbervilles* as an epic statement of this conflict in its simplest and most general mode, *Jude the Obscure* may be said to put, in a very similar form of art, a special case of the conflict; but a special case of striking and unavoidable kind. The mere "will to enjoy"—the fundamental motive of personal existence—becomes the more complex and more dangerous "will to power": the familiar phrases come pat for summarizing the difference between the two books. With Hardy's continual metaphysic in our minds, we may say that, while Tess only suffers her tragedy, Jude deliberately

EPIC FORM

courts his. She is punished simply for the sin of personal existence; but Jude, with the more rebellious consciousness of masculine nature, adds to this the further sin of aspiration—he being thus typical of his sex, as Tess is of hers. For the first requirement of feminine nature seems to be, on the whole, the *maintenance* of personal integrity (this desire typifying itself in purity, chastity, virginity); masculine nature, however, strives to increase the range and power of personality, to meet circumstance by offence as well as defence; but is liable thereby, through excess, to weaken personality, to become *unchaste*, to take some mixture of the brute world it attacks: Jude himself is an instance. Thus it is profoundly right that the more general tragedy, the tragic situation of which all others are specializations—the failure passively to maintain the integrity of personal existence against the main force of the world—should be a woman's tragedy; but that the life of a man should figure the special case of this essential tragedy—the courageous futility not simply of resistance, but of aspiration, of the desire to make circumstance give way to, as well as allow, personal being. It cannot be said that Tess's opposition to the power of the world is less brave or less vigorous than Jude's; but it is static; her prime desire is to be allowed to exist in her own pure nature. And as soon as she clearly perceives that the world has finally got the better of her, that her nature has been invaded by some influence of the worldly enmity which, unlike her first contamination, is not to be dislodged, which, indeed, turns her nature into something no longer *her own:* as soon as she is assured of this, she takes such vengeance on the world as will make her own destruction inevitable. Rather than to be on such terms, she prefers not to be at all. It is not thus with Jude. He has the bodily chastity of any ordinarily clean-minded man; but he has nothing of that intense spiritual chastity which makes a tragic matter of Tess's violation by the world. Jude will endure worldly contamination that Tess could never tolerate; so long as there is still some force uncrippled in him, able to keep up his assault on circumstance, he will go on, contaminate or not. It is only when he is no longer able to attack the world that he willingly dies. And without absurdly forcing sexual difference, it seems justifiable to take these two novels as giving a typically feminine and a typically masculine embodiment to the same tragic conflict of personal against impersonal.

The form which this conflict takes in Jude's history is beyond question a thoroughly epic conception. There is a certain simple grandeur,

EPIC FORM

as well as deep human and symbolic reality, in this assault of a single working-man on the high privileged towers of scholarship; for even when Jude turns his aspirations to religion, it is still scholarship he desires; he would be, somehow or other, a clerk in the old meaning. But, simple as this central theme is, and wide as its symbolic significance appears (a modern legend of man's unending hunger for knowledge), it is yet in itself more complex, and less general in its significance, than the theme of *Tess of the D'Urbervilles;* since it is aspiration instead of mere resistance. And with this there goes noticeably a greater complexity in the narrative substance which this theme possesses. It is not that the substance is here compounded out of a larger number of elements; on the contrary, the excellent, though somewhat subdued, comedy, and the splendid natural setting, of *Tess of the D'Urbervilles*, have scarcely any counterparts in *Jude the Obscure*. It is a book whose tone is as nearly uniform, from start to finish, as may be. But compensation for this comes from the remarkable elaboration in the psychology; the relations between the chief characters are of the subtlest kind, and described with keen and penetrating nicety; and out of this intricate relationship proceeds naturally a subsidiary second theme—a war between love and marriage—which is intimately woven in with the first. Jude himself is a transparent character, but by no means a simple one; though he has the apparent simplicity which comes from a single over-ruling passion, flowing through him like a strong electric current and infecting all the metal in him with one pervading magnetism. The whole of his nature is fascinated into a single desire; and his imagination lives always in its accomplishment, never in the difficulties before him, or in the embarrassment such a desire must cause to a life like his. Thus his desire inflames his imagination, and that again still more inflames his desire. When he sees, from a hopeless distance, the vague light which marks where Christminster, the city of learning, lies under the night, his imagination instantly conjures up the vision of Phillotson inhabiting the glowing town, "promenading at ease, like one of the forms in Nebuchadnezzar's furnace"; and at once despair becomes impossible for him, the desire is fiercely alight again. Through living in this continual aspiration, his nature seems to have no cross-weaving in its texture; all the fibres of his being seem laid to one direction. But this simple regularity is only his surface. When aspiration fails, a terrible perversity takes its place, which causes him deliberately to debase himself. If he is not worthy to subdue his fate, he will see to it that he is as unworthy as a man may be. This is fine psychology ; such perverse consolation for failure is the only possible consolation for him. At least it would make his life not a mere negation, but a positive thing, a life that never could have succeeded ; and so regret may be stifled. And of a piece with these transient but destructive moods, is his fruitless determination, after repenting of his frenzy, to mortify his intellectual desires by dedicating himself to a life of humble hidden Christian effort. And when he hopes to find in Sue Bridehead " a companion in Anglican worship," it is but a commandment given by his concealed nature, ironically speaking in the language familiar to his ruling desire, the only language his consciousness willingly listens to.

The device which the power of the world uses to oppose, or rather to ambush and capture, the assaults on circumstance of Jude's aspiration, is that terribly obvious one, *the flesh*. The world need put no subtle stratagems in train against such an attack as Jude's: it has but to remain unperturbed, and Jude will work out his own damnation. For this aspiring nature of his is lodged in worldly substance ; and thus, for all his desperate efforts to belong wholly to his own desires, secretly and profoundly he belongs to the world. Striving to effect his own motion, he is yet not only immersed in, but is himself an inseparable part of, the great onward motion of whole existence; and it is only the fierce unavailing imperative of his own desires that makes enforced obedience to the general flux of things an evil for him. To earn a living, mate with a woman, and get children—these are the things which form the natural scope of his being; and these are what the substance of his being compels him to do, like it or not. But through his aspiration to live outside this natural scope, these harmless things, holding him back, become his fearful evil. As you please, you may either say that his aspiration sins against nature, or that nature sins against his aspiration; but, one way or the other, there is sin inevitably, and punishment of sin:

> "The common food he doth
> Sustain his soul-tormenting thoughts withal,
> Is honey in his mouth
> To-night, and his heart, to-morrow, gall."

Jude is by no means one of those many-tempted souls who cry out desperately, "Before a pack of deep-mouth'd lusts I flee." It is simple nature that pursues him; and the story has to work out how the common nature of his being overtakes and treads down his aspiration—how two women, and the love they are ready to give him, become, through his insatiable need to strive against

EPIC FORM

circumstance, the *sins* for which he must be punished. In these two women, and their relationship with the finer faculties of Jude's mind, the real tragedy is placed; and they are drawn with as minute and scrupulous accuracy, and hold as important a position in the main theme, as Jude himself. The book therefore has a decidedly richer humanity than *Tess of the D'Urbervilles;* and for this very reason it has also perhaps a less tremendous mastery over the reader's emotions than that bare tragedy; for tragedy is somewhat mitigated, when attention is curiously employed with psychology. Moreover, aspiration is a thing more obviously punishable than mere desire for personal integrity, which was Tess's chief fault; and the catastrophe therefore falls less heavily. But the two books are entirely alike in the ruthless forward driving of their theme, and their superb shapeliness of unity; and it is only for personal preference to choose between them, if any choosing be required.

The story of Jude's relations with his wife Arabella and his cousin Sue Bridehead develops into a secondary conflict in which marriage *minus* love is opposed to what theologians call " unhallowed union " *plus* love; and this is mixed with a satirical discussion, thinly veiled in narrative, of the notion that an external ceremony can ratify love. Both Jude and Sue, with their repeated half-humorous, wholly reluctant, attempts to get themselves married, become indeed instances of the exact opposite notion; that love, namely, is safer without a contract of perpetual obligation. All this subsidiary matter is worked up with such elaborate care, that there are moments when the book seems in danger of becoming a problem-novel. But reassurance soon follows; and those frivolous theorists, who hold that art should be a place for debating social institutions, must be as little satisfied with *Jude the Obscure* as with the rest of Hardy's work. For this troublesome question of love and marriage comes in as inevitable incident of the main story, a necessary consequence, not otherwise important, of the psychological premisses. The whole point of the business is, that Jude's marriage with Arabella and his illegal love for Sue were equally ruinous to the achievement of his desire. His disaster is, that he has anything to do with women at all; for the fashion of his nature is such, that no woman can be to him anything but a representative of that great assimilating power of the general world which is his spirit's enemy—since it is all for holding him back from realizing *himself*. Either of these two women would have been an efficient agent of this; with the pair of them, Jude is simply devoured. But they as deeply contrast, the one with the other, in spite of their kinship in Jude's destruction, as any other opposed pair of women in Hardy's novels. Their manner of contrast, too, is of the kind he usually describes; but employed here in a completely new fashion—merely to show, you might almost say, that any kind of woman would be the ruin of Jude. Arabella is plainly the simple-natured, instinctive woman; in a rough classification, she would go with Marty South; but only in so far as she is contrasted with delicate, fastidious, clever, capricious Sue Bridehead. For in Arabella, the feminine instinct is sheer unquestioning destructiveness—at least, so it becomes by reason of Jude's nature. The only thing that concerns her is to get possession of a man, and to be possessed by him; and when Jude is the man, this means simply that his striving personality is fallen helpless into the mercilesss rapture of main, impersonal existence. Unquestionably, as a type of the women rudely called "man-eaters," Arabella is a masterpiece. Whether she is a wanton girl, or Jude's wife, or the publican's wife, or a "volupshious widow" weeping with anxiety to get Jude back again, this stupid, not unkindly, clumsily unscrupulous woman seems a creature charged with sinister and incalculable potency. And so she is; she merely transmits, and she has not enough personality to disguise, the power of the world against which Jude has pitted his spirit. I know no character in fiction who has a trait of such grim significance as Arabella's trick of sucking in her cheeks so as to give herself engaging dimples.

Arabella as a representative, as far as Jude and his aspiration are concerned, of *woman as sin*, is clear enough. Sue Bridehead becomes this only as a result of the most intricate psychological subtlety. At first she seems just the one woman who might "save" Jude—save him in the Wagnerian sense. She is as clever as Jude is, and, though clear-sighted enough to be sometimes tenderly amused at his unceasing dream, sceptical of the value of scholarship, and still more so of theology, she yet entirely sympathizes with his unfaltering desire. And she is amazingly lovable. None of Hardy's most charming women, not even Marty South or Bathsheba Everdene, can compare with Sue, for the strange and elusive delicacy of her charm. But she cannot escape her sex. The Christian ideal of purity, to be gained by the denial of life, disgusts her; she is for the pagan ideal, the simple unquestioning acceptance of life, neither banning sex nor exaggerating it. So far, the girl who, in that admirable first hint at her

EPIC FORM

character, buys casts of Greek statues, and loses herself in an innocent, theoretically voluptuous, worship of them, who "hates Gothic" and "likes the sound of Corinthian," is a merely consistent character, delightfully imagined. But her pagan purity is not such a simple matter as she herself considers it. It is her nature to excite desire, but she has a fastidious horror of physical sex; and rather than endure her husband with her at night, she jumps out of the window into the street. She desires to live altogether above the reach of sex; and yet she cannot help making a sexual appeal to men. But this fastidious hate of sex seems really to be the form taken in her consciousness by a concealed superstitious fear of the mysterious powers of existence. So long as this remains concealed, she is quite willing to be a rebel, and requires only her own self-approval. But even so, she has explained things by a not very comfortable metaphysic;[1] she has imagined "that the world resembled a stanza or melody composed in a dream; it was wonderfully excellent to the half-aroused intelligence, but hopelessly absurd at the full waking; the First Cause worked automatically like a somnambulist, and not reflectively like a sage." Such ideas come very near to a fear of existence. And when the

[1] The *form* of her metaphysic anticipates that of *The Dynasts*.

grisly catastrophe happens, the fear comes out of its concealment, and has its own way. She has deliberately opposed part of the prescribed order of existence; and she has fearfully suffered. These two things become causally connected; they become, that is, sin and its punishment. She must repent; which means that, having been broken, she must enjoy her brokenness, and, if possible, add to it. So she must leave Jude, and go back to tortured submission to her husband; and it is nothing to her, absorbed in the fearful passion of penitence, that to leave Jude is to hand him over to Arabella and damnation. Without doubt, Sue's character is the subtlest and most exciting achievement of Hardy's psychological imagination.

The story as it progresses has an accompaniment of emotional significance as obvious as that of *Tess of the D'Urbervilles*. But the indignation with the tragic fashion of existence is not here hot and flaming, but cold and bitter and almost cynical. It is brought into disconcerting prominence by being personified in Jude's son, one of the most daring, and certainly one of the most dreadful, imaginations in literature. This horrible boy seems unconsciously aware of the whole dismal past of human existence, and seems also to see nothing in the future but endless repetition of the same futility of suffering. But his

EPIC FORM

part is not merely one of gratuitous commentator; the action of the story takes its final tragic turn from his interference. That interference of his is a thing of such nightmare horror, that it depends simply on the mood in which one reads of it or thinks of it, whether it is to seem appalling or only grotesque. At any rate, like the boy himself, it is not easily forgotten; and, as a matter of technique, one can only be astonished at the way the mood which surrounds the whole story is concentrated into this formidable small boy, and, by his means, inextricably woven into the narrative texture. Even so, however, this formal condensation of the mood is not enough to counteract the tremendous emphasis it takes from being so personified. The emphasis is too great for the form of the book as a whole to contain. The mood breaks out, not quite unmanaged, but by no means completely mastered; it "chews the bit and fights against the reins." There has been a weakness of artistic control; and, when such perilous stuff is to be dealt with, it is only by a triumphant and utterly unquestioned mastery over the substance that art can properly be said to achieve itself. Here, in spite of notably skilful imagination, the art has undertaken to express something which it cannot quite command; and this is even more obvious in the few exclamatory remarks the author puts in, as it were, on his own account. The result, in all these passages, is not tragic art, the noblest thing man has within his power; not the bringing of life in its most threatening aspect into firm obedience to man's finest desire—namely, into perfect *form*—with the consequent turning of fearful matters into exaltation for the spirit. Such half-controlled art merely effects diatribe and invective; and it has scarce anything for the spirit but dismay and offence. But *Jude the Obscure* is a book that can afford occasionally to commit this fault; that it can do so, is the clearest testimony to its greatness. To its amazing insight into human nature, and to the terrible cogency of its tragic motion, is added a shapely grandeur of formal unity which, in the whole, is little disturbed by the flaws in its artistic control; and which makes it one of the most illustrious things in modern literature.

Throughout this discussion of Hardy's fiction I have simply assumed the metaphysic which is the ultimate matter of his art, without attempting in any way to examine it as a "truth." I conceive that to be no part of my business here; it is nothing to criticism, whether one considers the basic metaphysic of artistic expression to be a true or false, an agreeable or disagreeable, representation of the manner of our existence in this world. We may leave that to philosophy or religion. But it must be true to the artist, as long, at least, as he is in his art. And it must, for the reader, be a tenable, plausible, and coherent speculation, even when liberated from the art which holds it. So much is axiomatic. But the real question is, whether, by causing his version of life to relate itself closely and naturally with his metaphysic, the artist attains to that complete formality which is internal, intellectual, and emotional, as well as external, the shapeliness of technique; whether, moreover, this formality reaches beyond the stuff of familiar experience, to embrace the rarer experience, the consciousness that life belongs to *some* absolute reality. Thus, by reducing the whole *sense of living* to some formality, some shapeliness of significance, life attains, in the art, to mastery over itself; it makes itself what it profoundly desires to be, a manner of existence which is measured and proportioned; and while we are immersed in the art, the mere sense of living becomes the delighted sense of a perfectly masterful living If a metaphysic can effect this, it is justified; and the metaphysic of Hardy's art unquestionably does effect this. Only in this way, it seems to me, can the value of an art be fixed to something firmer than opinion: to fix its value to the "truth" of its conceptions, the pleasantness of its tone, or the usefulness, moral or otherwise, of its purport, is only to make it endlessly debatable. But the interests of moral usefulness and complete formality will not often be in opposition—they certainly are not in Hardy; for genuine morality is but a kind of shapeliness.

No great poet can do without a metaphysic: but that does not mean that it must always be explicit. Creative literature divides itself into two main kinds; that in which a metaphysic is fitted to experience, and that in which experience is fitted to a metaphysic. The first kind is the work of the poet who judges instinctively; the second, of the poet who judges intellectually. The two types have been described, once and for all, by Coleridge, in the persons of Shakespeare and Milton:

"While the former darts himself forth, and passes into all the forms of human character and passion, the one Proteus of the fire and the flood; the other attracts all forms and things to himself, into the unity of his own ideal. All things and modes of action shape themselves anew in the being of Milton; while Shakespeare becomes all things, yet for ever remaining himself."

It is only an accident that, in the contrast thus personified, the instinctively judging poet is dramatic, the intellectually judging is epic. There is no connection between this division and the *kind* of form; for if we compare English poets with Greek, it is evident that Milton must go with Æschylus, Shakespeare with Homer; not the two epic poets together, nor the two dramatists. Hardy in his fiction uses forms which may reasonably be called both dramatic and epic; but throughout the whole of his work, he belongs clearly to the army under Milton. He does not become the life he deals with, but compels it all to become himself, to fit in with a constant manner of intellectual judgment; and not only life, but even our enjoyment of life, he forces to submit to this judgment; and so his art is one which sorts well with the increasing self-consciousness of human nature. There is no rational possibility of preference for the one or the other of these two kinds of literature. In them we must only see two methods of arriving at one end—formal mastery.

VII

THE POEMS

HARDY's poems were originally brought out in three collections: *Wessex Poems, Poems of the Past and the Present, Time's Laughingstocks*. There is a continuous process of development in them. If we go through the three volumes in this order, it will certainly at first appear that the poems are attractive chiefly because of their authorship; they are facets of an unusually interesting mind somewhat awkwardly illuminated. The novelist versifying himself is not often a success. He is apt to think that the skill habitual to him will serve his turn in poetry, if only he adds to it a little concern for the laws of metre; and Hardy's earlier poems seem only one more negative proof, that nothing requires a more patiently specialized skill than poetry. But if we persevere in reading these pieces of interesting thought and strict external form, combined, on the whole, with unexciting, unpoetic language—language that neither stirs imagination nor gives living

THE POEMS

shape to the substance—we shall come to perceive that a somewhat novel kind of poetry is beginning to emerge out of the general failure; and in several pages of the second volume, and in most of the third, it becomes evident that Hardy has made a genuine addition to English poetry; he has brought a decidedly unusual idiosyncrasy both of substance and of method into fine artistic control.

It is interesting to see how this has come about. In the chapter of "Characteristics" it was noted that Hardy's diction shows, in the main, deficient apprehension of the concealed energies in language—of its "potential." The deficiency is plainly much more serious for poetry than for prose. It is possible for prose to rely entirely on the logical value of words, leaving the potential to take care of itself; so constructed, indeed, it can, in a narrow scope, do quite admirably. But poetry cannot be constructed merely out of the logic of language; some conscious management of the potential in words, of their nameless excitations, must go to its making. If one who depends, through choice or necessity, almost wholly on the logical or kinetic value of individual words, wishes to make poetry, there is only one way open to him; it is Pope's way. He must be scrupulous and ingenious to attend to the potential which is

THOMAS HARDY

the property not of individual words, but of *patterns* of words; only the pattern can save him from prosing. Great poetry will not result; for the manner of great poetry must certainly use the potential, the excitation, of words themselves and of patterns of words simultaneously. But a hard, straightforward diction, of value predominantly logical, enclosed, almost as if in some transparent case, in an aura of the potential energy that is derived from a continuous, repeating pattern of accent and rhyme—this may have a quite notable effect. The pattern, however, must be rigidly maintained. It can scarcely be modulated without endangering the delicate quality which keeps such poetry just on the right side of versified prose. It is always, in fact, a ticklish matter for this kind of writing to justify itself. If it fails to be poetry, why was it not set down as honest prose? For when the pattern is unable to do its required work, it is felt simply as an inconvenient misfortune; as here:

> But Buonaparte still tarried.
> His project had miscarried;
> At the last hour, equipped for victory,
> The fleet had paused; his subtle combinations had been parried
> By British strategy.

And yet, at the beginning of this poem, the pattern promised remarkably well:

THE POEMS

    In a ferny byway
    Near the great South Wessex Highway,
  A homestead raised its breakfast-smoke aloft;
The dew-damps still lay steamless, for the sun had made no
  skyway,
      And twilight cloaked the croft.

But Pope himself, for all his lifelong practice and the nicety of his talent, failed often enough to give his verses any real warrant of their pretence to poetry; and we ought not to be surprised that Hardy, whose poems have only been a bye work of his artistic life, is in them more often disguising prose than transmuting it. He has, however, one very great advantage over Pope; his thought, whether its expression justify the form given to it or not, is always considerable for its frankness and originality. Let him treat of the tritest or most ordinary thing, he will give some turn to the treatment that will repay attention. It need hardly be said, that it is only in the principles of poetic method that there is any suggestion of comparison with Pope at all; in genius, temperament, characteristic thought, the two are as unlike as may be. But in poetic method, it seems to me that Pope's example is of some critical value here.

Hardy, at any rate, whether instinctively or consciously perceiving the necessity for him, is extraordinarily careful to maintain exactitude of pattern—rhyme, metre, and stanza. His skill in keeping each poem to one firm consistent mould is evident from the first, especially as the mould itself is usually conspicuous for some intricacy; a thing which is also necessary, if words of such simple kinetic force are markedly to acquire the potential of poetry. In his later poems, the maintenance of uncommon pattern is done with wonderfully deft precision; and when the pattern is a common one, he is fond of enhancing it by such tricks as keeping a single rhyme regularly sounding throughout a poem's whole length; in one instance, through thirty-two stanzas. The artistic purpose, conscious or otherwise, of all this is never anything like bravura; it is mere necessity,—except for the few poems written in dialect, like the delightful *Fire at Tranter Sweatley's*, the only surviving piece, it is said, of a deal of youthful versifying. Where dialect occurs, the same access of potential in the words themselves happens as was noted in the case of Hardy's prose. For the rest, however, it is mainly from their strict and evident pattern that the words have to derive that heightened vigour which is absolutely necessary for poetry; as far, that is, as technique is concerned. For in those pieces where something genuinely poetical does unquestionably

THE POEMS

come off, it is pretty easy to see that subject has had as much to do with it as pattern. There are two main classes of subject in which Hardy achieves a real and even excellent poetry. Both of them, it appears, make this possible by reason of the intense fusion and concentration of thought which they promote. It seems that they are a kind of subject which cannot be connectedly thought out without such heat of intellect as will automatically burn up everything that is not absolutely required by the idea for its statement. And if we glance at the obvious failures, it is plain that this poetic method of Hardy's is most liable to break down when it is dealing with the not quite essential, with the slightly superfluous detail.

Besides the indubitable failures and the not less indubitable triumphs of Hardy's poetic method, some mention must be made of those fairly numerous pieces which may roughly be called epigrams; things hovering between prose and poetry. They usually versify some curiosity of thought, some reflection from the unexpected aspect of things, some ironical comment on life and death, rather insistently elaborating the favourite theme of Donne's preaching, that "all our life is but a going out to the place of execution." Such verses as those on *Shelley's Skylark*, pondering the fate of that "little ball of feather and bone," "that tiny pinch of priceless dust"; or as those that lightly warn us not to judge a man's character nowadays by his house (*Architectural Masks*), are certainly pleasing and, somehow, memorable, slight things as they are. Occasionally the irony is given some modest form of fiction; as when the architect refuses his client's whimsy for spiral staircases, on the ground that they would prove inconvenient for the handling of her coffin. Or it is expanded to considerable length, without losing its originating epigrammatic quality; as in *My Cicely* or *The Souls of the Slain*. The latter poem is a characteristic instance both of Hardy's unexpected reflection and of a style to which it is equally difficult to give or to refuse the name of poetry.

The poems wherein Hardy's idiosyncrasy of thought and style unite in undeniable, though not unqualifiable, achievement, are those which reveal either the philosophical or the psychological artist; and of these the latter kind is certainly the greater. It is scarcely possible to give lyrical form to abstruse metaphysical speculation, which is neither pure faith nor pure scepticism, without discovering that what is convenient for the art is inconvenient for the philosophy. The profoundly purposeless energy of existence; its terrible limitations, compared with what, in our fantasy, it might have been; the unalterable pace of what Hardy excellently calls its "rote-restricted ways" (suggesting thereby one of the most remarkable of modern scientific ideas—that what we call the physical laws are strictly the *habits* of matter): all these may be very impressively put into lyrical form by the device of addressing such conceptions under the name of God. But even while æsthetic appreciation is acknowledging the result to be serious and moving, philosophy can hardly keep quiet: "If these things trouble you, why increase their trouble by calling them God? Surely even art must perceive that these disturbing conceptions are the work of human wit and sense, and that, if God be at all, it is a million to one He is altogether outside any reach of wits and senses which the mere close needs of evolving life have fashioned?" Some such objection is unavoidably aroused by Hardy's lyrical attribution to the Deity of the humanly perceived limits of existence; and art which can be so easily questioned, though by something exterior to art, is scarcely to be called perfect. Nevertheless, the whole process of worldly existence, as we must to-day conceive it, is nobly and courageously brought before us in these poems; exhibited with austere, unflinching severity not only to our minds but also to emotion. This sort of thing is decidedly impressive, in spite of anything strict reason may say; the creatures of the earth are supposed to be speaking:

> Has some Vast Imbecility,
>   Mighty to build and blend,
>   But impotent to tend,
> Framed us in jest, and left us now to hazardry?
>
> Or come we of an Automaton
>   Unconscious of our pains? . . .
>   Or are we *live remains*
> *Of Godhead dying downwards, brain and eye now gone?*

The notion in the italicized words is one of those inventions in artistic metaphysic which can do without, and even go against, the approval of reason, because they excite in us the sense of vague, notorious feeling finally reduced to vivid and unique form.

There remain those poems which I have spoken of as the work of eminently psychological art. Here there is nothing that provokes cavil; æsthetic satisfaction has no need to excuse itself to philosophy. They are not narrative; Hardy's poetic method requires for its best success something more concentrated than narrative. They are momentary dramas of passionate or ironical human event, in which the ardent emotional essence of character or conduct is so fined down and intensified, that it needs but to be stated in some undecorated vigour of language, masterfully controlled into pattern, to become unquestionable poetry. It is poetry which, for its power of showing the spirit of passionate action instantaneously dramatized, cannot be closely likened except in some of the old ballads, in some such disturbing instance of tragic psychology as that famous one, "Edward, Edward." Passion, however, is not the invariable rule here. These sudden declarations of human nature in quintessence are sometimes merely ironical, as in those good-humoured gibes at systematic morality, "*The Ruined Maid,*" and "*The Dark-Eyed Gentleman.*" Occasionally the drama has a symbolic air; a good instance is the "tale" called "*The Supplanter*"—for, as in the ballads, Hardy's lyric sometimes approaches narrative without actually reaching it. In this singular poem, a man goes to lay memorial flowers on the tomb of his beloved, but yields to the enticings of the cemetery-keeper's daughter, who is celebrating her birthday with "wines of France" and a ball at the cemetery-lodge. He leaves her, and she has a child by him; next year, when he returns to accomplish "his frustrate first intent," he finds the cemetery-keeper's daughter wandering, an outcast, among the tombs with her baby. This time, she tries to make his pity come between his dead love and himself. But he flings her off:

> He turns—unpitying, passion-tossed;
> "I know you not!" he cries,
> "Nor know your child. I knew this maid,
> But she's in Paradise!"
> And swiftly in the winter shade
> He breaks from her and flies.

There is a certain terrible reality in the action of this fine ballad; but evidently its scene is no cemetery in the actual world, but one that lies in some strange district of the imagination; the reality is that of a symbol. A poem whose reality is even further removed from actuality is the ballad of "*The Well-Beloved*," wherein a lover meets a wraith which turns out to be his own idealization of his beloved. He would marry the wraith; but

> She, proudly, thinning in the gloom:
> "Though, since troth-plight began,
> I've ever stood as bride to groom,
> I wed no mortal man!"

The danger for Hardy in this kind of lyrical symbolic drama lies in the fact that it does not necessitate an absolute concentration of subject; we are apt to get such inept lines as these, which occur a verse or two above those just quoted:

> "O fatuous man, this truth infer,
> Brides are not what they seem."

THE POEMS

There is something of the tight-rope walker's risk in this method of his; the least slip, and a fall is certain.

But most of the poems in the class I am considering do not transcend the manner of actual life; not, at least, by revealing some symbolic parallel in imaginary regions. Actuality is transcended in them only by being fused and molten into glowing intensity. Their momentary drama requires a psychology purified from accidentals, completely at one with itself; and Hardy's method is in consequence assured of good success. The reading of these poems leaves a firm impress on the imagination. It is not their form that survives in memory. The form is seldom beautiful in itself; it keeps itself strictly to its necessary function of empowering the gist of the poem with the potential which poetry requires. That it performs this function is plain from the way memory is forced to lay hold of the gist; but that memory is at the same time willing to let the form itself slip, shows that this poetry is not of the highest order. No great poetry will leave us remembering what it said unless we also remember a good deal of how this was said; the how and the what are, indeed, inseparable. In Hardy's lyrical poems they are separable; his method is such, that they could not be otherwise. Nevertheless, though not of the highest, his psychological poems (to give them a handy label) are of a high order; their effect on imagination and emotion sufficiently declares that. The woman who, hearing they are bringing home the corpse of her husband suddenly killed, has her first grief for the untidiness of her rooms, but afterwards dies of a broken heart; the man who traduces the honour of his dead love in order to do her daughter good; the lover who suddenly finds his innocent beloved had once abetted a murder and sent a man to the gallows; the trampwoman who, in a whim of angering her fancy-man, is blasted by the result, again a murdering and a hanging; the barren wife who, after longingly awaiting her absent husband's return, quietly leaves him to the woman who will bear him a child; the mother who desperately medicines a betrayed daughter with an infamous brew, causing her death just as the seducer announces his repentant desire to marry her;—these tense dramatic figures, with their tragic and significant spirits revealed in a sort of instantaneous light, are not easily forgotten. Imagination knows itself the richer and the wiser for them. The poems are thoroughly modern, too; their persons do not belong to romance or story, but to recognizable, everyday species of the present; and the turn of the

THE POEMS

psychology, though comment and moralizing are avoided, frequently implies some typical modern questioning of received notions. The whole body of the poems of this kind will perhaps include twice as many as those to which I have alluded; several are not obviously tragical, some have a humorous twist. But they stand out pretty clearly from the rest of Hardy's poems, and form a natural group; and they are poems which, it seems to me, deserve a special place in our literature.

VIII

THE DYNASTS

LIKE most great poems, *The Dynasts*, it appears, does not owe its peculiar significance to the intention in which it first originated. Thomas Hardy, as *The Trumpet-Major* and several poems and short stories show, was early attracted by the "vast international tragedy" of Napoleon; and it occurred to him that there was room for some large imaginative treatment of the theme, which should at last give England her proper part in that hurly-burly.[1] The notion shaped itself into an immense spectacular poem, or "panoramic show," dramatic in style, epic in progress and proportion. There was to be no great attempt at a close continuous linkage of the action; the scenes would present the most notable specimens of those thronging events which make the ten-year period chosen one of the prodigies of history; and common knowledge would supply a sufficient nexus for the whole. It would be, in fact, a chronicle play on a very

---

[1] See the Preface to *The Dynasts*.

large scale, taking its unity simply from the actual logic of historical events. That this was the originating intention of *The Dynasts* seems pretty clear from the author's preface. But in order, no doubt, to give an epic breadth to the action, a set of phantom intelligences, "impersonated abstractions," was invented to hover above the human business. Though these persons sometimes interfere in the action, thus taking the place of the regular supernatural machinery in epic processes, their main function from the beginning was apparently to utter supernal comment, which would summarize and intensify the affairs presented. Cervantes, in his "Numantia," devised a similar family of spirits to enhance the sheer artistic effect of a dramatic history of warfare; he has sufficiently explained his spirits' function: "I was the first," he says, "to represent the phantoms of the imagination, and the hidden thoughts of the soul, by introducing figures of them upon the stage, with the universal applause of the spectators." So in *The Dynasts* these imagined spirits stand upon the human action like a group of statues on a figured pedestal—a summation in immortals of the multitudinous mortal welter beneath. Already, then, the commenting group of spirits has done something remarkable for the drama; it has realized that large imaginative unity which the mere logic of events can only suggest; what was simply war, becomes drama. The function of Cervantes' spirits, his "phantoms of the imagination" and "hidden thoughts of the soul,"—Spain crowned with towers, War, Sickness, and Famine—practically stops here; and perhaps Hardy's first intention stopt here also. But in *The Dynasts*, out of this primary function of the Intelligences grows an artistic condition completely reversing that of the original conception; and it is because of this that the poem has its real significance. In the action of the phantoms, the mortal action has been altogether dissolved. The choruses of Pities, Ironies, and Years are by no means there in order to provide an illuminating gloss of reflective generalization on the rages of the Napoleonic wars; on the contrary, "fiercely the predestined plot proceeds," in order to provide these spirits with tragic entertainment and speculation. The final purport of the poem is not the artistic exhibition of the special material borrowed from history, exaggerated by the supposed interest taken in it by a set of spiritual commentators; but it is the artistic exhibition of a philosophy, or rather of an attitude to existence—philosophy or attitude being typified in these spirits, and served by the vast action which they watch with a chance of exact expression, of showing how its theory, or mood, frames when applied interpretatively to a concrete mass of events. The poem does not fail thereby of being a spacious chronicle-play; on the whole it is certainly the grandest of all imaginative dealings with the last of the Titans and his tremendous affairs. But it is much more than this. It is the characteristic poem of our age; and characteristic in a profound fashion that has not been lately achieved by poetry among us—in the fashion of its philosophy. That is putting the case with only verbal convenience, perhaps. Philosophy is a useful word; but apt to turn awkward when used for poetry. The great characteristic of *The Dynasts* is, that in it we have artistic *formation*, definite and explicit, of the reach of man's present consciousness of the world, of his conception of human and cosmic destiny, of mind's chief traffic with the surrounding existence as far as the inevitable and unsurmountable barriers. That is all " philosophical " poetry can mean. It must give certain *shape* to an æsthetic metaphysic, formulate in clear art some supposed relation of known and unknowable, whereby man may live. But there is no necessity that the formulation, the metaphysic, should have to submit itself to a strictly philosophical scrutiny. Such a poem as *The Dynasts* with its opportunities of discoursing at large, easily avoids the fault noted in the corresponding lyrical poems, the fault of affronting philosophy. But this does not mean that *The Dynasts* may be treated like a sorites. The relation of known and unknowable is matter for emotion rather than for reason; and what this poem achieves is the presenting to emotion of a metaphysical idea held in some consistent and noble shaping. And this idea is one that underlies most of the intellectual life of our time; though the shaping is altogether the poet's own. Hardy, in *The Dynasts*, attains to something that the age of Tennyson and Browning quite failed to effect.[1] We can only say (but of course it must be said without proposing further comparison) that this epic-drama of Thomas Hardy's is, in what may be called its conceptual poetry, akin to the works of Milton and Wordsworth in our literature, and beyond it to "Faust" and "Prometheus Bound."

It is certainly not, however, the figuring of Napoleon in *The Dynasts* which suggests its comparison with the conceptual poetry of Satan, Prometheus and Faust. Napoleon is

[1] Though Matthew Arnold comes near to effecting it; Swinburne also curiously near, in such poems as the *Hymn of Man;* and Emerson's poetry (if we may count him in) nearest of all,—but of course he had the advantage, for a writer of that time, of not being an Englishman.

only one of "Earth's jackaclocks," concerning whom we are warned at the beginning of the poem, that in order to enjoy their drama we must just pretend them to be "not fugled by one Will, but function-free"; it being from the start perfectly clear, outside this pretence, that there is no room for anything "function-free" whatever in the rigid monism of the whole poem. And it cannot be by denial, but only by extreme artistic assertion, of an individual free will, that those vast, symbolic figures may be created, in which poetic formulation of the human mind passionately relating itself with the unknowable is at its supremest, because most inescapable for our emotions. Zarathustra, for instance, the youngest of these symbolic figures, is a glorification of free will in the midst of a metaphysic which, like Hardy's, makes free will inconceivable; the supreme illusion and the supreme disillusion co-exist in him, the former being required for an overwhelming formulation of the latter. It is interesting to note how Hardy, the artist, is so compelled by the logic of monism that free will can have no place in his poem; whereas Nietzsche, the philosopher, cheerfully puts the two incompatibles together. And it is interesting to note further, that both are justified artistically; Nietzsche by the splendour and anger of his formulation, Hardy by the simplicity and gravity of his.—It was not therefore possible for the subject of *The Dynasts* to be a human or Titanic figure immensely symbolizing the conceptual poetry; this latter must itself be the direct subject of the drama. So is it also with Wordsworth's greatest poetry. But Hardy has nothing of Wordsworth's extraordinary compensation; his amazing fusion of abstruse idea and perfect poesy, so that it is no flourish of admiration, but simple truth, to say that what Wordsworth means can only be expressed in the language he himself uses. Of Hardy's inability to write with anything like the noble manners of those other poets I have mentioned, there need be no discussion. Nevertheless, it is only with the work of such poets that *The Dynasts* can be profitably compared.

The Dynasts, then, is a play within a play. The structure is, perhaps, a little troublesome to attention. The inner play, the chronicle, seems at first too exciting, too massive, to be properly enclosed within the other; and there is no doubt that the easiest way to read *The Dynasts* is to skip everything printed in italics—the surrounding, supernatural drama, that is. It is sometimes desirable, for the purpose of artistic enjoyment, to ignore a good part of the poet's purpose. The person, for instance, who is scrupulous to work out the moral allegory in

THE DYNASTS

"The Faerie Queene" at every stage, will certainly not enjoy it so much as the person who simply loses himself in the poem's beauty. Although to read *The Dynasts* merely as a great chronicle-play would be to miss the real significance of the whole thing, it might conceivably be maintained that the poem, so read, becomes artistically more enjoyable. That this is conceivable shows, I think, an imperfect structure; no one could conceivably maintain that "Paradise Lost" and "Prometheus Bound" do not become artistically the more enjoyable, the more the moral significance of Satan and Prometheus is understood. But though this attitude to *The Dynasts* is conceivable, to read the poem with scrupulous attention to the poet's whole purpose is very far from confirming it. The effect of the supernatural drama is, certainly, somewhat to dehumanize the historical drama; but it is surprising how Hardy manages to exhibit the vast human action as being "fugled by one Will" without making it uninteresting. And the inevitable dehumanization, caused by the poem's simple, rigid fatalism, is easily outweighed by the fascination of watching how this huge, clamouring turbulence of mortal affairs is firmly shaped into a great concrete symbol of the ideas proposed and questioned in the surrounding supernatural drama. What the character of Prometheus, in fact, is in "Prometheus Bound," the Napoleonic chronicle is in *The Dynasts*. But by symbolizing the fundamental purpose in the fortunes and character of a single superhuman figure, an absolute fusion of the conceptual poetry and the whole embodiment is possible; Hardy might have achieved this, if he had taken for his symbol Napoleon instead of the Napoleonic chronicle. In his poem, the symbol and the things symbolized cannot be perfectly fused; at best they can only have a closely concentric, but always separate, discussion. But, unquestionably, it was more in accord with contemporary notions to take a mass of events as a symbol rather than a single person; and the resulting extraordinary gain of novelty and originality may very well compensate for some loss of artistic perfection. Moreover, Hardy's wonderful sense of form achieves such a finely concentric shaping of his human and superhuman material, that at the end of the poem each has become formally, if not substantially, merged into the other.

This seems the place to consider briefly two more general accusations which have been brought against *The Dynasts*. The first is merely theoretical. The poem is in the form of a play; but it is not for the stage. The belief that this statement is a paradox is probably derived from Wagner. It is curious that a musician, who proved his notion of dramatic poetry to be a shapeless hullabaloo, and his notion of stage-setting to be the grossest Philistinism, should be taken for an authority in the æsthetics of drama. Yet Wagner's æsthetic speculation often has a stimulating quality. It is, however, apt to fly off into theoretical vapouring, of which his contention, that dramatic writing must always be meant for stage performance, is a type. His prestige has undoubtedly gained for this idea a good deal of support of a frivolous kind; Hardy himself has thought it worth while to notice in his Preface the resulting objection to *The Dynasts*. The question, as he properly observes, "seems to be an unimportant matter of terminology." And, it might be added, that to condemn a drama as art because it is not meant for the stage, is to ignore astonishingly the actual facts of artistic experience. It is to ignore the fact that man can read. For, through being able to read, he has added to himself a special faculty for visualization; and the man for artistic theory to consider nowadays is a man possessing this faculty and giving it æsthetic exercise. Poetry was instant to take advantage of the faculty as soon as it appeared; and there can be no real reason why dramatic poetry should be excluded from an advantage derived from something which is now an integral part of human nature. The spoken word must always remain the prime material of poetry; the thing is, that the poet can trust a cultivated reader to supply mentally the spoken word to the written. And when it comes to the action of drama, obviously this visualizing faculty, due to the habit of reading, can do things quite beyond the range of stage performance. It enables Hardy to show his reader the whole of Europe at one view, "as a prone and emaciated figure, the Alps shaping like a backbone, and the branching mountain chains like ribs, the peninsular plateau of Spain forming a head"; to show also "the peoples" of this Europe, "distressed by events which they did not cause, writhing, crawling, heaving and vibrating in their various cities and nationalities"; and then to fill the scene with "a new and penetrating light, endowing men and things with a seeming transparency," an anatomy which reveals "all humanity and vitalized matter" as a single organism urged by the primal impulse. Why should this be improper in art? Why should the great formal advantages of dramatic shape be confined to plays capable of being staged? The matter, perhaps, need not be considered further. But it may be remarked, that when we read "Pro-

THE DYNASTS

metheus Bound," and when we read *The Dynasts*, our brains work in precisely the same way; the fact that "Prometheus Bound" was originally a stage-play is, artistically, no concern of ours whatever. Yet the theorist who condemns *The Dynasts* would never think of passing the same sentence on "Prometheus Bound" merely because the latter *has been* staged. That sufficiently shows the absurdity of this theory. It is not its fitness for the stage which makes drama good; but it is the presence in it of certain formal virtues which makes drama good for the stage or good for reading, or good for both. That a play on the stage may be more impressive than a play in an arm-chair, is another matter altogether; but that does not mean at all, that the visualizing faculty of literate mankind should not possess its own kind of drama.

A thing, however, which may be more seriously objected to *The Dynasts* is that it preserves unnecessarily a convention which belongs merely to the writing down of stage-plays—the practice of putting dialogue in verse, direction in prose. Strictly, drama, whether on the stage or in the arm-chair, consists in performance. The performance of a stage-play is made up of spoken words and visible action; but since action cannot be written down, the poet gives a few notes in prose roughly to indicate what he designs. But in a play intended solely for mental performance, there seems no reason why this convenience should persist. The written poetry of the dialogue has to provoke the mental performance of spoken poetry; which, again, is only a means of conveying the characters and feelings of the persons. But if poetry is on the whole a more potent means of doing this than prose, why not employ it also for the stage-directions? These have to provoke a mental performance of the action; and surely for this, as for dialogue, the most efficient medium would be poetry; especially when the directions are as elaborate and significant as those of *The Dynasts*. The poem in scope and substance takes notable advantage of the freedom possible in purely mental drama; but it has not tested to the full the capabilities of this kind of literature. That remains to be done, by putting the whole of it—dialogue, action and setting—into poetry.

But as a matter of fact, the prose directions of *The Dynasts* are just as vivid and provocative as the poetry. This leads to the second general objection to the poem—to the quality, namely, of its verbal poetry. To the discussion of Hardy's verse in the last chapter, little need here be added. *The Dynasts* is not a poem

THE DYNASTS

to be read for beautiful or imaginative phrasing. It is in the thing as a whole that its poetry consists; the splendid formal mastery which holds the three parts in one firm unity carries up fine prose and indifferent verse alike into something superior to themselves. But apart from the share every line has in the cumulative poetic effect of the whole, there is not much to be said for the verse of *The Dynasts*. The metre does certainly add energy to the language; but the movement of the blank-verse on the whole is not work that would be tolerated by a poet who had studied his craft as a painter studies his. The choruses show much ingenuity of stanza-formation without as a rule achieving any beautiful music; though certainly the ironic choruses frequently go to a tune that wonderfully renders a gibing cynicism. The diction has some fine touches of such athletic concision as this:

> He's scarcely old,
> Dear lady. True, deeds densely crowd in him;
> Turn months to years in calendaring his span;
> Yet by Time's common clockwork he's but young.

That is admirable phrasing. But the reader has to endure a good deal of this sort of thing:

> Nordmann has fallen, and Veczay: Hesse Homberg,
> Warteachben, Muger—almost all our best—
> *Bleed more or less profusely!*

THOMAS HARDY

There are, however, a few moments of splendid language in the poem; in particular, the magnificent Chorus of the Years, anticipating Waterloo, at the end of Act VI of Part III. There is an indescribable solemnity in this chorus, prophesying the effects of warfare on the harmless, insignificant inhabitants of the battlefield—coneys, moles, hedgehogs, larks, snails, worms, butterflies—coming as it does between the furious human perturbations of Ligny and Quatre Bras, and the inevitable climax of the whole tragedy, Waterloo. Just as the violent business of the human action seems almost getting beyond the control of its symbolic purpose, there comes this chorus, not minimizing, but enlarging, the threatening enormity of the climax by its catalogue of minute catastrophes; to the impassive spirits of the years, life is a web of such single weaving that the crushing of the tunnelled mole under the cannon-wheels is of the same account as the sabring of the gunner; it is all part of the same eternal, relentless, useless purpose; the endless tragedy which the coming battle has to symbolize is not humanity's, but vitality's. The short chorus suffices to bring the perilous excitement of the chronicle back into symbolic control; it is a notable instance of Hardy's formal power, as well as of the faculty which proves

THE DYNASTS

him a great visionary poet, the faculty of giving to imagination a fiercer reality than the actual world. And here, and in a few other passages, the language is equal to the visionary grandeur of the whole poem.

But, once more, it is the quality of the poem as a whole that gives *The Dynasts* its commanding station in modern literature. The double drama is thoroughly organized into unity; but in order to effect any summation of the poem's whole quality, we must first attend to the outer circle of drama, to the phantoms. These spectres, to whom the drama of human events is presented as a symbolic school for their affections, beliefs, and general attitude to existence, are themselves dramatic formations of man's mind, or rather of man's modern consciousness of the world. The middle place of this phantom drama is held by the Ancient Spirit of the Years and his train of choral attendants. He has the voicing of the profound essential in man's latter-day conception of the universe; he is the consciousness of monism, of the single urgency driving all the manifold shows of being. To him, too, belongs insistence on the necessary consequence of strict monism; namely, that the huge, boundless turbulence of the world can effect nothing outside itself; it can have no final result, for this would be something that is not the existing world. It would be an addition to existence, and a strictly monistic world can never do anything but simply go on being the world; its turbulence is for nothing but to be turbulent. In modern poetry this conception of the final uselessness of existence (except for what it can make of itself —truly an important exception), has its first clear expression in Leopardi,[1] though Lucretius, that prophet of modern thought, all but expresses it. In *The Dynasts* it is the basis of the whole matter. The play begins with the idea:

> It works unconsciously, as heretofore,
> Eternal artistries in circumstance,
> Whose patterns, wrought by rapt æsthetic rote,
> Seem in themselves its single listless aim,
> And not their consequence;

and at the end of the whole vast business, the Years can but return to the fundamental scepticism. What is the use, the good, of it all? It is still " indovinar non so ":

> O Immanence, that reasonest not
> In putting forth all things begot,
> Thou build'st Thy house in space—for what?

[1] Poi di tanto adoprar, di tanti moti
d'ogni celeste, ogni terrena cosa,
girando senza posa,
per tornar sempre là donde son mosse;
uso alcuno, alcun frutto
indovinar non so.

The sentiment might do for the motto of Hardy's idea of tragedy. It is not inappropriate to observe that the notion is not,

THE DYNASTS

But man's consciousness of his world can never be simply an intellectual failure to find any ultimate significance in existence. Accordingly, the phantom Spirit of the Years and his attendants are flanked on either hand by two other groups, the Pities and the Ironies. For the Spirit of the Years, the world simply exists in its own unalterable nature; its immense processes go on for ever without any reference to supposed good or bad. He is a sublime intellectual apprehension, neither liking nor disliking. But the Pities and the Ironies are not intellectual, but emotional; they are man's profound, inescapable desires for some sort of significance, or purpose, in the world. They are the Optimists and the Pessimists. But note that their optimism and pessimism are direct reactions from, not facile accompaniments of, their emotional attitudes to the spectacle of existence. The Pities find the show a horrifying tragedy; so horrifying that they conclude there *must* be some kind of good at the end of it all. The Ironies, on the other hand, take existence as an enjoyable comedy; but they can only do so by enjoying the perfection of the malice which they suppose is at the bottom of the world's affairs. The Pities'

in itself, pessimism. Pessimism is not the denial of significance, but the assertion of evil significance.

belief that a good must somehow result from such a dreadful business as existence, is only the natural desire to escape from reality into the shelter of an ideal, though it be one "pinnacled dim in the intense inane." But the delighted pessimism of the Ironies may seem fantastic. It is not that really, however; nothing is more certain psychologically, than man's perversely pleasurable excitement by what goes counter to his notions of rightness. To enjoy the worldly spectacle because it seems managed by a purpose of deliberate cruelty, is the sublimation of this perversity. The queer complexity of modern consciousness could not be better exhibited than in these spirits of tragic optimism and amused pessimism.

There are other phantoms in the supernatural drama; but it is these three groups, the Years, the Pities, and the Ironies, that supply the drama with its action. The action is of the simplest kind; but very important for the poem's meaning. Neither Pities nor Ironies can understand the purely intellectual, one might say scientific, interest in the world which is all the Spirit of the Years, unmoved by any feeling, allows himself. It is arranged, therefore, that the whole family of spectres shall watch the affairs of earth for a while, the Pities expressly hinting that a close view of suffering humanity

THE DYNASTS

(Napoleon being in his fullest power) will compel the Spirit of the Years to adopt their sentiments; the Ironies falling in with the scheme, and by their subsequent remarks showing that they too believe the Spirit of the Years must at last forsake his detachment and enjoy the comedy of infinite malice. "Old Years," as the Ironies sometimes call him, consents to sit out an act or two of the human drama, suggesting, however, that he already knows the plot, and is not likely to be moved to pity or irony by it. But before the play begins, he reveals, by a supernatural light which dissolves material opacity, the spiritual anatomy of earthly life; the exhibition is repeated several times later on, always with the same purpose. Throughout the seething complexity of human passion and action run innumerably the fine impulses of the single, original urgency, like nerves charged with currents of will. Nothing human, nothing whatever, moves of itself, but everything merely accepts the irresistible commands of primal energy, which is imagined as a thing in the nature of Will—the Immanent Will. Every existing thing, in fact, not merely obeys the Will, but is actually part of the Will itself, which exists forever in the sum of its parts, and forever "overrides its parts." And as the action proceeds, it becomes evident that the Will has no object except to go on willing. But neither Pities nor Ironies accept this. They continue to suggest to the Spirit of the Years that this or that bears them out, is tragic or comic, must be condemned or applauded, shows signs of eventual good or continual malignity. To all these suggestions the Spirit of the Years answers by placidly demonstrating their absurdity. The purpose of existence is neither good nor bad, but simply to exist. There is nothing more to be made of it. He allows the spirits to interfere in the drama of humanity if they choose, to speak to the characters in warning or temptation: " Speak if thou wilt whose speech nor mars nor mends."[1] He has been so long watching the unalterable working of the " unrelaxing Will" that he has got beyond liking it or disliking; he can only observe. Nay, they themselves, the phantom intelligences, are as firmly in the power of the Will as the men they watch; they can only observe, pity, or sneer as the Will allows them. Except for the universal fatalism, there is no conceivable existence. But as the Spirit of the Years is unchanged by the weaker spirits, so these are unchanged by their stern monitor; they are Pities and Ironies to the

---

[1] But sometimes, as will be noticed shortly, he forgets himself, and credits their interference with real effect. After all, this Spirit is a figure in the human likeness.

THE DYNASTS

end. The Pities even relieve their feelings by chanting, when the play is all over, a hymn, not to the Will as it evidently is, but to the Will as they still think it ought to be; this is idealism!

But unquestionably, the artistic effect of the whole poem is that which the Spirit of the Years recommends to his underlings. For this Spirit is the essential characteristic of the modern idea of the world; he is the ruling consciousness of the time; and the business of the poem has been, in spite of the double revolt of feeling of the Pities and the Ironies, to set forth at large his intellectual apprehension of universal existence. It is the biggest, the most consistent and deliberate exhibition of fatalism in literature. The enormous tormented spectacle of the Napoleonic wars has been represented, not as a complex of human purpose governed by a presiding fate, but as a system where there is neither being nor doing which is not fate itself. No purpose, great or small, moves through the mass of human event, except the single purpose which drives existence onward. Nothing whatever has been, or ever could have been, attained, but the continued action of the Primal Will. The huge process of human agony and triumph has no function in itself; it is only the eternal Will uselessly uttering existence. It is true that there appear now and then some obscure hints that the existence caused by the Will may have some reacting result in the Will itself; in effect, that it may learn from experience, for, strictly, it is only its own experience that the Will can ever cause. Man being part of the Will, his sense of the tragic pains of being may somehow induce the Will to be not utterly indifferent to the pain it causes in its creatures. The last words of the poem express this; the Pities hope, and even believe, that the Will may at last become infected by their sentiments. But this comfortable tag, this giving the last word to the Pities and their baseless idealism, has a very slight effect compared with the purport of the whole poem.

Thus extracted, the conception of a world so rigidly monistic seems too simple to be profitable either to art or philosophy. But the immensity and variety of its working out in the poem very easily justify the conception here. In the common business of thought it may be best to neglect an idea of such paralysing simplicity; but in *The Dynasts* it appears as the one thing to which everything else must somehow be related; there, without doubt, it is a most formidably impressive reality. The whole poem is designed to aggrandize the conception. Europe appears as "a crinkled ground"; armies look like caterpillars; Napoleon an insect on a

THE DYNASTS

leaf. Material and spiritual detail is persistently belittled, in order that the whole may appear greater. Earth is only a microscopically verminous mote among "the systems of the suns," and their "many-mortaled planet train": the assertion is not meant philosophically, but æsthetically, to enlarge the vastness of background to human endeavour, a background filled with infinite manifestations of one unalterable fatalism.

But now we are come to the real artistic significance of *The Dynasts*. I have previously said that this poem is a great summation of the significance of the novels; it deals directly with what they powerfully suggest. The thing is, however, that *The Dynasts* does not make explicit that which is implicit in the novels, by merely stating at large a philosophic idea of existence exemplified in a huge tragedy. The idea itself, for all its explicit appearance, is mastered by the condition of art; it is presented, that is to say, not as a philosophic idea, but as a *tragic* idea of existence. Monism is a notion sufficiently familiar to anyone nowadays; we are not here concerned with its claims to be considered as a "truth," only with the fact that it governs the modern consciousness of man's temporal destiny. But in art an idea of the world must be treated exactly in the same way as the appearance of the world; it must be controlled into some significantly acceptable *shape*. For, to revert to the argument used in the second chapter, an idea of the world, like appearance of the world, is the work of the formative power or desire inherent in mind, uttered in the one through intellect, in the other through sense; but in both the utterance is imperfect. The function of art is to perfect the utterance of this formative principle in man, to give its power complete achievement, to satisfy its desire. A grievous story will become tragedy, and therefore profoundly enjoyable, if its embodiment be so managed by art as to give that sense of order, coherence, significance—in fact, of perfect shapeliness—which is the triumph of man's formative desire. The problem is precisely similar for an idea. The monism of *The Dynasts*, extracted and nakedly stated, is assuredly not an enjoyable idea; just as the bare plot of a tragedy is not likely to be enjoyable. What the poem, then, has to do is to effect some artistic formation (which will probably be felt as ethical significance) of the relations between man's perceived experience and the cosmic conception of monism. The Pities and the Ironies both represent ineffectual attempts to fashion into significance the processes of a monistic universe. Some formation as definite as theirs, but less scholastically ethical, is required; and to supply their

THE DYNASTS

failure is, perhaps, the main business of the poem—certainly the most notable thing in it, except the excitements of the chronicle history. The primary, single energy of the monistic universe is conceived as a Will, an Immanent Will. The notion is so obvious nowadays, that we are apt to forget that this is itself an æsthetic formation of an idea into a shape of thought familiar to consciousness, and so easily appreciated. But the next thing required is to give familiar, appreciable, definite form to the relations between human experience and this ultimate Will; in a word, to explain—but artistically to explain—the nature of the Will. It is important to insist that the Will supposed throughout *The Dynasts* is not a philosophic, but a tragic, metaphysic. All the innumerable processes whereby this Immanent Will of Hardy's utters and articulates existence, it has long since got by heart; it is concerned with nothing but this habit of multitudinously existing. Whether the habit began in consciousness or not, we may think as we like; as things are now, the habit is grown to such perfect precision that it has lulled the Will into a drowse, wherein nothing is active but the habit itself. The joys and agonies of the existence it causes are nothing to it; the mere habit of causing existence is everything. There is neither good nor bad purpose in the universe; it just goes on and on in a sublime routine—"wrought by rapt æsthetic rote"—for no other purpose than to keep the routine going on and on.

As a philosophy of existence, it would be very easy to say that this will not do. As a tragedy of existence, it is surely magnificent, a profoundly enjoyable shapeliness of idea, nobly familiar to the desires of consciousness. The formation is not absolutely uniform throughout the poem; but the same kind of shape is kept consistently in all its variations. Here are some of its most admirable formations:

> So the Will heaves through space, and moulds the times,
> With mortals for Its fingers! We shall see
> Again men's passions, virtues, visions, crimes,
>   Obey resistlessly
> The purposive, unmotived, dominant Thing
> Which sways in brooding dark their wayfaring!

"Moulds the times with mortals for its fingers!" This is great *modern* poetry; artistic formation of humanity related with our ultimate conception. Even visions "obey resistlessly"; but that which they obey is "unmotived" though "purposive." But of subtler thought is the following account of "in-brooding Will" with its "sealed cognition":

> In that immense unweeting Mind is shown
> One far above forethinking; purposive
> Yet superconscious; *a Clairvoyancy*
> *That knows not what it knows*, yet works therewith.

THE DYNASTS

That gives to the Will the state of ecstasy—and the state has seldom been better described. The passage is the finest of the more abstract formations of the Will, unless we except the splendid phrasing of:

> The all-urging Will, *raptly magnipotent.*

Of the versions of the Will in more concrete imagery, the following will serve as specimens.

It is habitual handicraft:

> like a knitter drowsed,
> Whose fingers play *in skilled unmindfulness,*
> The Will has woven with an absent heed
> Since life first was; and ever will so weave.

A magic lantern:

> So let him [Napoleon] speak, the while we clearly sight him
> Moved like a figure on a lantern-slide.
> Which, much amazing uninitiate eyes,
> The all-compelling crystal pane but drags
> Whither the showman wills.

The Spirit Ironic thinks that:

> The deft manipulator of the slide
> Might smile at his own art;

but the Chorus of Years replies:

> Ah, no: ah, no!
> It is impassible as glacial snow.
> Within the Great Unshaken
> These painted shapes awaken
> A lesser thrill than doth the gentle lave
> Of yonder bank by Danube's wandering wave
> Within the Schwarzwald heights that give it flow!

THOMAS HARDY

Again, in the magnificent Ironic Chorus over Austerlitz, the Universe is a fermentation, the Will its chemical energy:

> Stand ye apostrophizing that
> Which, working all, works but thereat
> Like some sublime fermenting vat
>
> Heaving throughout its vast content
> With strenuously transmutive bent
> Though of its aim unsentient?

These will suffice to show the character of the tragic metaphysic to which monism has been reduced. But there is one matter which refuses to accept tragic formation, and appears as mere horror. It is pain:

> the intolerable antilogy
> Of making figments feel.

This is the great injustice; and one which, perhaps, is incapable of artistic control. The Pities complain of it from time to time; they cannot endure that men, the puppets jerked in the Will's heedless drama, should "feel, and puppetry remain"; agony should give them the right to independent being, or should never have been devised. This is naturally rebuked by the Spirit of the Years. Pain was not devised; it just unhappily occurred. But his explanation, which invokes crude accident, "luckless Chance," is the very antithesis of artistic form; it is the negation of form, admitted disorder, therefore not tragic. The matter could not have been avoided; but the poem must be praised for but rarely touching the "intolerable antilogy" of human pain.

To have discussed *The Dynasts* thus far, with only the most general allusions to its historical drama, will doubtless have offended the opinions of many readers, who are properly enthusiastic for the splendid qualities of the huge chronicle play. Had I wished merely to give myself "the noble pleasure of praising," I should certainly have taken the easy course of admiring the poem as a superbly adequate exhibition of the greatest period in modern history. But I wished rather to appraise the poem's extraordinary significance in contemporary literature; and it is more in the outer circle of supernatural commenting drama, than in the inner Napoleonic play, that this significance is to be found. Indeed, when this outer drama is understood, the symbolic significance of the subservient inner drama necessarily follows. At the end of the First Part there occur a few lines which should be noted; for they are, in effect, a glimpse behind the scenes of the play. A chorus of spirits sings these words:

> Our incorporeal sense,
> Our overseeings, our supernal state,
> Our readings Why and Whence,

THOMAS HARDY

> Are but the flower of Man's intelligence;
> And that but an unreckoned incident
> Of the all-urging Will, raptly magnipotent.

Yes, this outer drama of spirits is an imagination of man's own consciousness watching a characteristic spectacle of worldly event; watching it, questioning it, resenting it and acquiescing, and with difficulty and conflict deciding how much, and what, final significance there must be in it for him at this present stage of his growth. Man looks for reality as one looks for the bottom of a lucid, profound water; the transparency at length, through mere depth, becomes opaque, and his eyes never find the bottom, but only the limit of their vision. As the practice of existence continues, man thinks he can see further and further into the depths of appearance; yet his vision only pierces the transparent appearances to come at last on the opaque appearance. But until that opacity holds vision back, there is something in man which will not be satisfied; and perhaps the opacity comes now an inch or two deeper down than it did once. This craving vision in man, that will never be done with perfectly proving its own scope, has its phantom embodiment in the Spirit of the Years; it is for him to declare the depth of vision which the practice of time has given to man. The Pities and the Ironies are willing to stop their search

THE DYNASTS

when appearance becomes gloomy; there is always in man their scrupulous enterprise, ready to hold back when it seems convenient. But also there is always an unscrupulous enterprise; and this it is that continues from age to age, the Ancient Spirit of the Years. He will not stop for darkness, until it becomes at last impenetrable; and he forces along with him those unwilling other spirits into whatever depth of exploration he can attain. Thus, in the outer play of *The Dynasts*, man's present vision of the world is dramatized; man is both its subject and its composer; and the chronicle play, which, though much the bulkier of the two, is given as a show for the persons of the spiritual play, is significant chiefly by what it elucidates in these ideal spectators.—It would have been dangerous for the artistic firmness of the whole, if the poem had openly confessed, that not only are these seemingly immortal spirits the shapes of man's conscious experience, but the Immanent Will itself, their continual theme, is only the *form* man himself has given to the ultimate appearance of the unsearchable reality.

The two circles of drama are not geometrically struck. They touch each other several times. The phantoms, which æsthetically realize the poem's metaphysical purport, are allowed to interfere in the human action, though that should be only the subject of their gloss. The effect of one drama presented to the persons of another is, at each interference, momentarily lost; the phantoms become the regular epical supernatural machinery, directing the course of the action. Probably, however, there is considerable advantage in not too strictly maintaining the arrangement of doubled drama, which might look too much of an artifice. The chronicle play itself decidedly gains by these interferences, in acquiring epical proportions, which seem to require, however large the human affairs may be, some clear supposition that they are at least capable of arousing superhuman interest to something more than contemplation. So the Earth trembles when Maria Louisa consents to the match with Napoleon, and the shudder tumbles down and breaks a portrait of Marie Antoinette; for the spirit of the Earth excuses herself thus:

> When France and Austria wed,
> My echoes are men's groans, my dews are red;
> So I have reason for a passing dread!

This noticeably adds impressiveness to the action. And the superhuman interest is at times more actively interfering than this; the spirits, in order, at a favourable moment, to "impress" (their own word) Villeneuve, and keep him in a required determination, appear

THE DYNASTS

to him as white sea-birds, perching on the stern-balcony of his ship, and mysteriously watching him with piercing eyes. Again, they enter into assemblies and affect the action by influencing common opinion, spreading disquieting rumours. Yet there is certainly one difficulty in these interferences. The economy of the poem is injured by them; for in a poem so persistently elaborating a universal necessity, how can they be anything but patently superfluous? The action cannot go otherwise than it does; human and superhuman effort can never alter it or make its course more certain, can never do aught but carry out the inevitable. Yet even the Spirit of the Years himself, who should know better, urges Villeneuve to suicide. The phantoms, like the humans, might have been permitted the weakness of thinking to influence the process of destiny; but their interference, though slight enough, is apparently of real effect on an action which is used to symbolize absolute necessity in a tumult of events. We can hardly get over this by supposing that the necessity works by means of the phantoms in such cases; since the phantoms themselves are but abstractions of human mind shaped in art.

But the surrounding drama of spirits exercises on the chronicle play a more subtle and more general influence than these interferences. It is most easily noticed in the characterization. Those studies in exciting and curious psychology which are so remarkable in the novels have no place in *The Dynasts*. There are no sudden surprising revelations of individual will in the poem; no displayings of unsuspected capacity, which yet confirm the shapeliness of the character. It is not that this sort of thing would be out of keeping with a chronicle action; but simply that, in the presence of the supernatural drama, it would be artistically inconvenient. For each figure in the chronicle play must be simultaneously an individual will and a part of the will of general existence; the former must be a special exhibition of the latter. There can therefore be no question of individual *free* will; but characters can only reveal themselves in conspicuous psychology when they are intensely conscious of their own freedom. This consciousness would not, perhaps, be very troublesome to fatalistic philosophy; but in fatalistic art, any noticeable appearance of seemingly free psychology would be dangerous to the harmony. It was therefore wisely excluded. Indeed, the characters sometimes deny their own freedom. Thus, Napoleon:

> Some force within me, baffling mine intent,
> Harries me onward, whether I will or no.
> My star, my star is what's to blame—not I.
> It is unswervable!

THE DYNASTS

The Spirit of the Years commends him for this:

> He spoke thus at the Bridge of Lodi. Strange,
> He's of the few in Europe who discern
> The working of the Will.

That Napoleon should "speak thus" is evidently convenient for the symbolism of the whole chronicle; and it is moreover not out of tune with his character in history. But not thus may profoundly psychological drama be written. Similarly, though not often thus overtly, the main symbolic requirements of the play override and subdue the characterization of Pitt, Nelson, Wellington, and the other chief figures. But there is no reason why great drama should be dependent on exquisite psychology. *The Dynasts* is peculiarly able to dispense with it. The persons are figured in vivid and characteristic outline, their psychology is a matter not of delicate modelling and shading, but of firm, shapely lineament. And that is all we require; for the drama is sufficiently supplied with vitality from its amazing wealth of varied human material and the splendid resonant process of its events.

It will be sufficient to review very briefly the outstanding merits of the chronicle play; they are too magnificently obvious to need any critical labouring. I should think that the average cultured person in England will henceforth take his knowledge of Napoleonic history chiefly from *The Dynasts*, just as his knowledge of English mediæval history comes for the most part from Shakespeare's chronicles. The historical foundations of *The Dynasts* are said to be accurately laid; it is evident, at any rate, that they were very carefully studied. But the hard rigour of the imagination wherein this history is displayed, is the main thing; the formidable obscure mass of events, dissolved by an eager mind, has been thence crystallized out into a lucid substance of clear, true structure. Some foreknowledge of the period, as the preface says, is assumed in the reader; but a very little will do. Choruses of rumours bridge important gaps; and the others are easily jumped. The whole great story goes forward with a tremendous momentum; and also with the nicest precision. Battles and strategies, usually so troublesome to read about, are as clear as statuary groups in sunlight here. The tangled policies of the time have no doubt been somewhat straightened and simplified; their motives, subterfuges, calculations, and personalities have certainly been woven into a pattern which the reader can trace from start to finish without being baffled by its twisting and swerving and doubling. But it is not only the occurrences of Napoleonic warfare and policy which

THE DYNASTS

form the subject of *The Dynasts;* but also the whole temper of the period, the reaction of European society to those gigantic, rousing futilities. Men and women of all sorts pass through the scenes, royalties, courtiers, statesmen, soldiers, fashionables, merchants, business men and peasants; all preoccupied with the one prevailing enigma, which they themselves formulate in the great name of Napoleon, but which to the reader appears in an infinite change of formula, in the guise of every person that comes into the drama. Its free expatiation through the whole commonalty of human society is one of the great features of the poem. Since there is here needed not so much psychology, as the drawing of characters in clear lineaments, Hardy's usual difficulty in managing genteel figures does not show itself. The drama is terse and vivid, whatever kind of humanity it employs. The greatness of Napoleon could not be more intensely dramatized than in that brief but eager conversation of three sovereigns, wherein, after brushing aside Austria's claim to be the real defeater of Bonaparte, the rulers of England, Russia and Prussia in turn claim this distinction for their own countries; four short speeches sum up the character of France's tussle with Europe. Still, it is in the rustic scenes that the dialogue is most memorable;

chiefly because here Hardy uses that incomparable prose which he has fashioned out of the Dorset dialect. In such superbly vigorous scenes as that of the beacon-keepers in the first part, or of the effigy-burning in the third, the talk of the cheery, puzzled rustics more brilliantly portrays the bewildered events and relentless destiny of the time, than the debates of statesmen and the policies of kings. It is much the same with the battles. I suppose no reader will easily forget the vivid humanities of Hardy's battles; the great personal elements in war have never been more strongly seized, than in Napoleon and his marshals throughout, Nelson and Captain Hardy at Trafalgar, Kutúzoff in the Russian campaign ("his one eye staring out as he sits in a heap in the saddle"), Wellington in the Peninsula and at Waterloo. But for a picture of war that almost injures with its verisimilitude, we should rather remember that grim scene of the cellar full of deserters from Sir John Moore's army: "quaint poesy, and real romance of war," as the Spirit Ironic says.

As we watch the immense spectacle proceeding, we share the phantom's vision; here, by so easily providing us with faculties of superhuman largeness and penetration, the epic qualities of the poem take great advantage from its structure

THE DYNASTS

of drama within drama. The watching spirits, and we who watch the spirits, have the occasional privilege, already noted, of discarding the opacity of material shows. By this means, at Vittoria, there is exhibited "the electric state of mind" in the opposing soldieries, the vision "resembling as a whole the interior of a beating brain lit by phosphorescence." More usually, it is an unnatural scope of sense that we possess; we "see all things at one view." We

> Count as framework to the stagery
> Yon architraves of sunbeam-smitten cloud;

and land and sea fall so far beneath us, that Maria Louisa's progress from Vienna to Paris seems "a file of ants crawling along a strip of garden matting," and battle-ships float before the wind "like preened duck-feathers across a pond." But the effect of these enlarged powers is not always to belittle the parts, and so unify the whole, of the action. Often enough they wonderfully increase the impressiveness of the human business; the Russian campaign, seen from our balloon-like height of vision, is an unforgettable experience for imagination. We are not always in these altitudes; but the phantoms, when they contract their senses to a merely human range, have a wonderful instinct for selective perception, singling out just those features of the scene which most intensely characterize it and make it unique. Indeed, all the visionary part of *The Dynasts* is of astonishing quality, possibly the most exciting element in its substance. That in a poem which, as Mr. Oliver Elton says, "could only be in verse," the actual *vision* of it should, nevertheless, be almost wholly conveyed in prose, is a curious anomaly. But this has been already discussed; and, as it turns out, we certainly would not be willing to change the prose of Hardy's descriptions for the verse of his dialogue. Here is the cockpit of the " Victory ":

> A din of trampling and dragging overhead, which is accompanied by a continuous ground-bass roar from the guns of the warring fleets, culminating at times in loud concussions. The wounded are lying around in rows for treatment, some groaning, some silently dying, some dead. The gloomy atmosphere of the low-beamed deck is pervaded by a thick haze of smoke, powdered wood, and other dust, and is heavy with the fumes of gunpowder and candle-grease, the odour of drugs and cordials, and the smell from abdominal wounds.

Not many poets could better that for precision and selection.

There was at first, it appears, some difficulty in finding an audience for this extraordinary poem. I do not know how its popularity may stand now; but it is scarcely to be supposed, that a thing so vivid and great in its imagination, and, for anyone at all conscious of the finer issues of the time, so charged with gravity and significance, can long miss common acknowledgment as one of the most momentous achievements of modern literature.